WOODEN STARS

INNOCENT GEARS

WOODEN STARS

INNOCENT GEARS

MALCOLM FRASER

Invisible Publishing
Halifax & Toronto

Library and Archives Canada Cataloguing in Publication

Fraser, Malcolm, author
     Wooden stars : innocent gears / Malcolm Fraser.

(Bibliophonic 4)
ISBN 978-1-926743-40-0 (pbk.)

     1. Wooden Stars (Musical group). 2. Musicians--Canada--Biography. I. Title. II. Series: Bibliophonic ; 4

ML421.W886F84 2013   782.42166092'2   C2013-905674-2

Cover photo by Ian Fildes | ianfildes.com
Typeset in Laurentian & Slate by Megan Fildes
With thanks to type designer Rod McDonald

Printed and bound in Canada

Invisible Publishing
Halifax & Toronto
www.invisiblepublishing.com

We acknowledge the support of the Canada Council for the Arts which last year invested $20.1 million in writing and publishing throughout Canada.

Invisible Publishing recognizes the support of the Province of Nova Scotia through the Department of Communities, Culture & Heritage. We are pleased to work in partnership with the Culture Division to develop and promote our cultural resources for all Nova Scotians.

NOVA SCOTIA
Communities, Culture and Heritage

Canada Council
for the Arts

Conseil des Arts
du Canada

Dedicated to Stacey DeWolfe—my wife, best friend, first reader and loyal music listening companion through the years.

INTRODUCTION

My brother's first band was called Jerks at Play. They made
their racket in the basement of our Ottawa home, played a
few gigs at the junior high school, traced their name in the
dust on our car's back window.

The band didn't last long; the writing on the wall (for me
at least) was when their style evolved from fun, trashy punk
to terribly dark and serious metal, a transition marked by
the changing of their prospective album title from *Open Up
and Say "Fuck You"* to *Book of Shadows*.

The album was never completed—or, I don't believe, ever
even begun. But for a bunch of 12 and 13 year olds fucking
around, they were fairly talented; a number of the members
went on to become actual musicians. Perhaps the most notable aspect of the band was the presence of two drummers:
my brother Nick and another kid named Andrew McCormack. During JAP's cover of Zeppelin's "Moby Dick," the
lengthy drum solo (or duo, I suppose) was actually pretty
impressive, the two trading off fills that would have shamed
many an older drummer.

By the time high school came around, both Nick and
Andrew had undergone another musical metamorphosis,

from metalheads into full-on jazz snobs. And so a few years later, I was a bit surprised when my brother told me that Andrew had joined "some rock band" who were in talks to sign with Sub Pop. This was the early 90s, so the prospect of an Ottawa band joining the label who introduced Nirvana to the world was a big deal. I figured they were a grunge band and thought, "well, good for him."

This was my rather misleading introduction to the Wooden Stars, who would go on to make several albums, influence a later wave of musicians who decisively put Canadian music on the map, and become one of my all-time favourite bands (and just to throw my gauntlet down, I don't mean Ottawa bands, Canadian bands or 90s indie rock bands, but favourite bands period). Operating at a remove of several subgenres over from grunge, they had some connections to certain emerging tendencies in various underground scenes, but always stood out with their own sound.

I actually came pretty late to the whole indie rock thing— it would be another year or so before I got turned on to Pavement, Guided By Voices, Liz Phair and so on—but I think it's fair to say that I had a wider musical palette than the average 20-year-old.

When I was growing up, my parents—sophisticated listeners it would seem—kept the family on a steady musical diet of Beatles, Dylan, folk and jazz, forsaking the soft rock Top 10 (it would be years before I'd discover the joys of bands like Fleetwood Mac, the Bee Gees or ABBA). They eventually got into some cool contemporary 80s music like Talking Heads, which was the only band my whole family could agree to listen to on long car trips, resulting in an early immersion in their whole discography. The first music I got into of my own accord was "Weird Al" Yankovic and novelty songs, courtesy of the *Dr. Demento Show*, which I would tape on my Walkman and obsessively listen to, memorizing the goofy jokes and cultural references.

Then, at the age of 12, a Lebanese headbanger named Robbie "Boomer" Haddad turned me on to metal via Black Sabbath and Van Halen. This may have been the gateway to my first, greatest and most shameful musical love, Rush. I must have listened to the Canadian prog trio more or less exclusively for about three or four years, during the formative period of age 12 to 15.

No doubt this musically warped me for life, but at 15, I was saved by discovering the Ramones, immediately rejecting prog and casting my lot with old school punk. That led me to a love of post-punk and New Wave, in particular Devo, which then sent me down a whole other path of weird music—Captain Beefheart, Pere Ubu, and down various rabbit holes of noise rock, outsider music and so on. Meanwhile, through my brother, I cultivated a loose appreciation of free jazz and avant-garde music. I liked some "cool" bands like the Pixies as well as contemporary weirdos like Ween and the Butthole Surfers, but in general I was more interested in anything that was old and obscure.

When I look at this bizarre musical stratosphere of influence on paper, it's as though I was programmed to be a Wooden Stars fan.

What I prized above all was originality, and that's something they undeniably had. The band's singers and guitarists, Michael Feuerstack and Julien Beillard, developed an unmistakably unique way of singing and playing together, with beautiful harmonies complemented by interlocking guitar lines, the whole thing anchored by the unorthodox but solid rhythms created by Andrew and Julien's younger brother Mathieu (later replaced on bass by Josh Latour). Their songs' complex rhythms and intricate guitar lines were due to an amazing musical chemistry, a rare synthesis of self-taught outsider/punk sensibility and solid musical chops.

And though the lyrics were sometimes inscrutable, at their best they had the destabilizing force of a Buñuel, Jodorowsky or Lynch film. Striking poetic imagery sat alongside stark brutality and joyfully goofy absurdism, often in the same verse. At any rate, I defy anyone to cite rock lyrics as original and evocative as *The bomb squad woke from a dream of a planet without fire*, or *Daylight is dangerous, I save it in a deerskin flask when it drips from cows' tongues licked through the barn wall cracks*, or *Gold dust settles in the whites of your eyes. You say you only believe in love, but I only believe in fire.*

Quite aside from all that, the band had the rock-solid fundamentals of good pop music: memorable melodies, harmonies and hooks. While their music sometimes reflects the particular excesses of 90s indie rock, overall it holds up to the scrutiny of time and stands with the best music in the genre. They never made a bad record, and each album improves on the last.

"They were so ahead of their time," says Mocky, a fellow Ottawa native now based in Los Angeles and best known as a songwriter and co-producer with Feist, as well as a solo artist in his own right. "I think all the big indie Canadian bands owe them a debt of conceptualism and musicality."

While you wouldn't immediately infer an influence from the Wooden Stars' esoteric pop to Arcade Fire's angstful anthems, the latter band's Richard Reed Parry, Tim Kingsbury and Jeremy Gara were all part of the Wooden Stars' Ottawa circle. All three did time in Mike Feuerstack's solo project Snailhouse; the latter two were roommates with Julien and Mike, respectively, during the Wooden Stars' heyday, and cite them as a major influence. "I feel influenced by them for sure—my guitar playing and the way I approach songwriting," says Tim Kingsbury. "For a long time when I moved away from Ottawa, I felt that everything I wrote sounded like a Wooden Stars song."

So what is it that's so good about the Wooden Stars exactly? In writing this book I've had ample opportunity to consider that question, and the best answer I can come up with is this: There's music that simply satisfies you and makes you feel good. You might get that feeling from bubblegum pop, classic rock, hip hop, country or your personal favourite singer-songwriter. Then there's music that destabilizes you, challenges you, confronts you and (if you open yourself to it) broadens your musical horizons. You might get that from free jazz, contemporary composition, extreme noise, experimental techno or outsider music. The list of artists who can do *both* these things is very short. And the Wooden Stars, for me at least, are at the top of that list.

Because of their weird, destabilizing elements, and of course because there's no accounting for taste, there are more than a few people who simply don't like the band. And whenever I defend them, I invariably get the answer "Well, that's because you know them," or "Yeah, but you're from

Ottawa." So let me clear something up. Although Andrew and Josh were good friends of my brother's in adolescence, and in later years Mike would become a friend and collaborator of mine, I was never close to the band during their glory days, in spite of all our social connections. As awed as I might have been by their talent, I was probably even more intimidated by the stern persona they projected in their dealings with the press. Though in person they were guardedly friendly, they also had a reputation for having sharp tongues and not suffering fools gladly.

Besides that, I didn't even live in Ottawa during the Wooden Stars' heyday. After graduating high school in '93, I got out of there as fast as I could. I was always a fan of the band, but not an up-close witness to their story as it unfolded. To the extent that they knew me at all, it was vaguely, as Nick's weird, uptight older brother.

All of that is simply to say that it's not as an insider, or some kind of Ottawa scene booster, but merely as a fan that I come to praise the Wooden Stars, and to explore their story.

The members of the band were kind enough to share their versions of that story with me. (Mathieu and Josh proved difficult to contact, but late in the writing process after repeated attempts, they both answered some questions by email, with Josh providing a follow-up by phone.) It's been two decades now since the story began, and so some details are remembered differently by different people, while some are forgotten completely. "I feel as though I'm trying to recall a movie that I watched 20 years ago," says Josh. "I still have the visceral feelings from the movie, but very little recall of the minute-to-minute unfolding of the story."

The band members are also acutely aware of the disconnect between their indie-icon status and the stark reality of their inability to break through to a bigger audience. In our conversations they were unrelentingly self-deprecating, sometimes brutally so, as much about their music itself as the twists and turns of their career. But there was also a lot of laughter and affection as they discussed the journey of this totally singular band.

CHAPTER 1

Hidden Decorations

"In our early days, we had a lot of negative reinforcement.
And so I think that galvanized our resolve to be the weirdos
that we were." – Michael Feuerstack

I don't remember the first time I listened to the Wooden Stars' debut album *The Very Same*. Nor do I remember buying it, although memories of going to record stores and purchasing other seminal albums remain burned, along with various other random details and unnecessary detritus, in my mind.

Maybe it would help if I knew when the album came out. With a perverse obscurity that's typical of the band, they didn't list the release date on the album. Wikipedia says 1995, while Mike Feuerstack's website claims 1994. Nobody else seems to be able to confirm either way.

In the greater scheme of things I suppose it doesn't matter, but it's frustrating when key details like that slip into the ether. In my group of friends I'm known for having a photographic memory for useless trivia, but the photos are starting to fade. I'm pretty sure it was '94, if only because I remember seeing the band for the first time that summer and recognizing some of the songs.

At any rate, I do have strong memories of listening to the album. On the opening track, "Farewell to the Yellow Jacket Avenger," two odd yet compelling voices sing this peculiar couplet combining gentle lyricism and abrupt absurdity:

When I was just a ray of light
All your songs came back to haunt you
The reindeer on their stilts approach you
In nightmares and in dreams.

The high harmony is fractured and frail, the melody barely in tune and vaguely menacing. The music is strange too: a simple piano melody, with beautifully cavernous reverb, contrasts a raw bass sound that would seem more at home on a lo-fi punk record, while the drums' soft shuffle has an unusual sonority (achieved, I would later learn, by dragging a metal chain across the snare). Besides all that, what kind of rock band opened an album with a ballad? This was unlike anything I'd heard before.

One of the Wooden Stars' defining characteristics is the difficulty they present in describing their sound. It's the first thing many of their contemporaries mention when recalling their first exposure. In the early 90s, Ottawa musician Dave Draves was working at a music equipment store called Songbird. As in any city, the store was a hub for both fresh-faced novices and jaded scene veterans. At this kind of job "your daily routine is to basically ignore any sort of noise," says

Draves, and yet he couldn't help but notice one day when two young kids were jamming in the store. "I thought 'what are those guys playing?' It sounded like punk jazz—not to put a label on it, but it sounded really cool."

The makers of the strange sounds were Julien and Mathieu Beillard, two brothers still in their teens. Despite being well shy of drinking age, Julien had already logged some hours on the bar scene with The Roustabouts. I had gone to see them a couple of times because my friend Dom Salole (today known as Mocky), played drums for them. I remember them being kind of a loose, rootsy rock band; I didn't know Julien, and all I recall is that he had long hair and sang a pretty good cover of the Velvet Underground's "What Goes On."

Despite his youth, "Julien always seemed way older and more experienced as a musician," says Mocky, who also recalls that "he played with a purposefully dry, sharp, reverbless tone" and "was always writing things with really strange historical references."

"Oh yeah, I was a seasoned veteran," Julien scoffs when asked about his youthful scene presence. But Mocky and Draves weren't the only people to take notice. Julien also made an impression on Michael Feuerstack, a transplant to Ottawa from Moncton. Two years older, Mike was also a bit of a veteran; YouTube footage can be found of him in 1987, at the tender age of 15, screaming his head off with Moncton hardcore band the Underdogs (also featuring his friend Rick White, later of Eric's Trip and Elevator).

"I thought he was a weirdo, a great weirdo," Mike says of Julien with a laugh. "He was an amazing guitar player even then, as a teenager. And he's a really unique person, which comes through in his music—which is true of all the best musicians. He was just an amazing player with a totally unique perspective on songwriting."

Asked to describe this perspective, Mike struggles to define it. "It's really hard to put your finger on something like that. It's the same thing that draws you to any new thing: if it sounds unique to you... but it somehow strikes a familiar chord, or makes you feel feelings that you didn't know you wanted conjured up." This balance of familiarity and discomfort would come to characterize the Wooden Stars both musically and lyrically.

Though the two had met a few times—"he wasn't particularly friendly," Mike laughs—one chance meeting would turn out to be fateful. "I think he kind of recognized me and remembered that I was some kind of musician," recalls Mike. "And then he asked if I played drums, and I just said yes. I didn't have any experience playing the drums, but I wanted to play music with him." With this bluff successfully enacted, the duo formed a band called Rufus Wheeler, which lasted about a year.

During this time, whether by happy accident or latent savvy, the Beillard brothers found themselves making a music business connection. Amy Hersenhoren, today a talent booker for some of Toronto's top music venues, was then bartending to support her budding career as a band manager. Peter Murray, a high school friend of hers, dropped by her workplace with his young cousins, Julien and Mathieu.

"He left his cousins with me 'cause he had to go somewhere that didn't let minors in," she recalls with a chuckle. "We started talking about music, and their knowledge blew my mind. The stuff they were into was really sophisticated, and not what you would think a 15- and 17-year-old would listen to. Julien was talking to me about [avant-garde guitarist] Fred Frith, I think." When Murray returned to pick up his young charges, they left a Rufus Wheeler demo with Hersenhoren.

Meanwhile back in Ottawa, Rufus Wheeler was giving way to a new project. Though he'd faked his way into the drummer's chair, Mike remembers that "after a while, it just sort of became clear that I should switch to guitar." With Mathieu recruited on bass, the first version of the Wooden Stars was formed with drummer Dave Coyne.

This line-up produced the band's very first recordings, a never-officially-released cassette and a song called "Hate Everyone," which appeared on a compilation on the Raw Energy label in 1993 alongside notable "alternative" Canadian bands of the era such as Eric's Trip (featuring Mike's Moncton high school friends Rick White and Julie Doiron), Jale, King Cobb Steelie, Change of Heart and The Dinner is Ruined.

After about a year in the band, Coyne moved to Toronto. In need of a new drummer and at the suggestion of Mocky, Mike and Julien contacted Andrew McCormack. The first jam took place in the McCormack family basement. Andrew recalls only that "it was pretty obvious that we were all pretty nerdy."

Julien remembers that, "the first time we had a jam session with Andy, he told us that he didn't play backbeats"—referring to the simple 4/4 beat that's one of the fundamental roots of rock 'n' roll. "Just a policy, no backbeats," he adds with a kind of delighted disbelief. ("I think that might have been true," confirms Andrew with a hint of embarrassment).

"I remember being really excited by his playing, probably for that reason," Julien continues. "I like feeling a bit disoriented. That's exciting to me. And I never really played with a drummer who was like that."

It was equally unfamiliar territory for Andrew. "I knew it wasn't jazz and I was quite happy with that, but I also knew it wasn't rock. It sort of felt like a slightly exciting hybrid of experimental music being injected into rock. In hindsight, there's a long history of that, but I just wasn't familiar with Frank Zappa or a whole array of experimental rock musicians."

But though it was coming from a different place, the music intrigued the young drummer. "It was definitely unlike anything I'd ever heard," he says. "It was just obvious that there was a strange brew of Julien's unique guitar style and Mike's gift for songwriting. I wasn't totally sure if it was ever gonna work, but I knew there were enough ingredients that there was something interesting about it."

The band began to compose songs together, a laborious process of cherry-picking the best moments from marathon jam sessions. "More so than any other band I've been in, we would often begin our rehearsals by just jamming for like, an hour, two hours," laughs Mike. "It could be the worst kind of blues rock, but half of us are playing it wrong, and often parts would emerge that we would turn into songs."

Today when I think back to those early Ottawa days, it strikes me that it was a bit of an incubator of creativity. When I would go to punk shows, I'd see bands like Anal Chinook, a super-theatrical, conceptual yet obnoxious band whose lead singer Gavin McInnes and guitarist Shane Smith would later go on to found the multi-million-dollar

Vice empire. Across town, Tom Green was making ridiculous, hilarious videos for the local cable TV station that would later make him an MTV star.

Even in my immediate group of friends, the main points of interest all had to do with creative projects. Today, while not household names (with the exception of my classmate Alanis Morrisette, who was already a bubblegum pop star at the time), a decent number of us are making a living (albeit in some cases barely) as writers, musicians, actors, designers, comedians and so on. We were working toward it even then, and we were all just teenagers; it took me until much later to realize that most people's adolescence was quite unlike this thriving, supportive artistic milieu.

Mike, however, remembers the atmosphere differently. "We probably had kind of a chip on our shoulder—probably," he stresses with an ironic chuckle. "In our early days, we had a lot of negative reinforcement. A lot of rejections, a lot of audiences that didn't like us and a lot of promoters who wouldn't book us. We'd give our demo tape to other bands and say 'Can we open for you sometime?' and never got any response from any of that. And so I think that galvanized our resolve to be the weirdos that we were."

"The reaction was really mixed," says Geoffrey Pye, a friend and collaborator of the band whose own still ongoing project, The Yellow Jacket Avenger, inspired not one but two songs on the Wooden Stars' debut album ("Farewell to the Yellow Jacket Avenger" and "Song For the Yellow Jacket Avenger"). "Some people were really moved by their music, like myself and many other groups, and some people were really indifferent, viewed it as this sort of pretentious thing.

But I really don't think it was at all. I think it was really sincere, and people who didn't understand it were really stupid," he laughs.

Among those who did like them, the band inspired a fierce devotion. Friend and future band member Josh Latour remembers his first time seeing the band, at the short-lived but renowned punk space 5 Arlington. "The Wooden Stars were on the bill with a punk band," he recalls. "I think it was winter as I remember steam pouring out the exterior door when it was opened. The kids were packed into the room. I have a memory of them sitting cross-legged or pressed against the walls. It was like everyone was witnessing an atomic test explosion (minus the funny goggles). I had never experienced that kind of cultish feeling from seeing a show."

Though the band were never punk per se, they found a place in that scene, both because (as has always been the case for musical outsiders) it was the only scene that would have them, and because of their sometimes anarchic energy. "They could be punk. When Mathieu was in the band, they could be off the rails," says Draves. "Mathieu had this stage presence," recalls Stephen Evans, who at the time was working at the Carleton University campus station, CKCU. "He was very defiant-looking; he'd just stand and stare. He didn't do any bass player moves—he never did the 'bass neck,'" he laughs, bobbing his head in imitation. "He just stood motionless. It looked really defiant and aggressive."

Geoffrey Pye has similar memories of Mathieu's punk rock volatility. "Sometimes Mathieu would rip at his clothes or rip at the bass or start punching things. I remember the rest of them almost being in sort of a trance. It was very awe-inspiring to watch their first shows."

"At times it was unsettling," remembers Ottawa artist Wyatt Boyd. "The music would plunge into the most violent depths. I remember a show or two where they'd hauled a drum barrel on stage, which they then miked and smashed bottles into for terrifying percussive effect. This was around the time that Andrew mastered the art of scraping tones out of his cymbals as though they were giant singing bowls. Except they didn't sing—they screeched. Now picture all this happening while Mathieu screamed and quaked and lapsed into Vodoun-ish, out-of-body states... it was some scary shit."

The early performances also featured a lot of improvisation. "When they were in their element, they would improvise a good half of the set. At that time, nobody did that in the sort of alternative pop world," notes Draves. "I remember thinking the entire performance could fall apart at any moment, it was almost like they were up there on a wire instead of a stage," says Boyd. "There was so much tension generated from wondering if they'd be able to pull their own music off!"

"Because Andy still wasn't really playing backbeats, or only half the time, it was sort of an open question how a given song would be performed," says Julien, who remembers this approach leading to "a lot of disastrous performances, but also some really fun, inspired moments."

But as ramshackle as their shows could be, the band had a solid card to play in the business via Amy Hersenhoren, who continued to be a supporter of the band's talents. "Julien's guitar playing was incredibly sophisticated, and the interplay between him and Mike was unbelievable," she says. "And then when they got Andrew as a drummer—Dave Coyne was a good drummer too, but [Andrew] took it to another level."

Taken under her managerial wing, the band got opportunities to play outside of Ottawa and get some high-profile opening slots for notable Canadian bands of the time such as Eric's Trip, the Rheostatics and the Inbreds. Hersenhoren set up a label, Lunamoth, for the flagship acts of her management company, releasing a self-titled Wooden Stars 7" in 1994. She was also responsible for the band's biggest and most contentious brush with success.

"I started working for Sub Pop, doing press for them in Canada," she recalls. After the unprecedented breakout success of Nirvana and Soundgarden, the Seattle-based label was the single hottest name in the business, with even their furthest-afield acts, like experimental-metal kingpins the Melvins, moving on to major-label deals.

"Jonathan Poneman [Sub Pop co-founder] and I became friends, and he came to town to have a meeting with me one day," Hersenhoren recounts. "The day he was leaving, we went out for breakfast, and I gave him a copy of the first Wooden Stars cassette. By the time I'd gotten home from breakfast, he'd already left a message on my machine saying it was, like, the best band he'd ever heard."

What happened next is remembered differently by various players. While generously offering, "I don't wanna take all the credit for ruining it," Andrew figures that the more experimental rhythms he brought to the table were too weird for the label, who'd heard the band's demo with the more straightforward Coyne on drums. "So I think whatever Sub Pop liked about the band, I ruined. When they heard the new incarnation of it, they were no longer interested," he laughs.

The story that went around at the time, which Mike confirms today, is that Sub Pop wanted the band to work with a certain producer; when they declined for artistic reasons, the label withdrew its offer. "We just felt that if they wanted us, they could trust us to do something on our own, make our own choices about where to record and stuff like that," says Mike. "Looking back now, I don't see it as a problematic offer. But we didn't take it, because we didn't want to not do things the way we saw them. I don't really regret that, but at the same time, it wasn't that crazy what they were asking. They wanted to know who we were gonna work with, because they wanted it to come out a certain way that they thought would fit with their roster. That wasn't a very artistically liberated way of going about it for us," he laughs.

"We, slash Julien in particular," says Andrew, "were slightly ideological about what was right and what was wrong and how things should be done. Chances are it would have been a record full of compromises that we weren't interested in making. Julien was right in that sense; it would have been a record that he wouldn't have been into."

Hersenhoren, for her part, says, "I don't think I would wanna go on record saying what happened. It certainly wasn't anything that the boys did, but I think in the end they felt like they weren't on the same creative page." Whatever the reasons were, the aborted record deal sealed the Wooden Stars' reputation, either for supreme artistic integrity or self-defeating stubbornness depending on your point of view, as "the band that turned down Sub Pop"—much to the band's frustration and to the detriment of their relationship with the media.

"It's sort of typical of them to be of the attitude that no one was going to tell them what to do," says Dave Draves of the Sub Pop debacle. But the grunge giant's loss was his gain; he'd recently acquired some vintage recording gear, and wanting to set up a studio, he convinced the band to work with him.

CHAPTER 2

Innocent Gears

"It's a progressive rock album, but as if it were recorded by a high school stage band." –Julien Beillard

The Wooden Stars' first album, *The Very Same*, was recorded by Draves in exceedingly modest circumstances. "We helped him build his shed that he was building the studio in, and in return we'd spend a day recording stuff in the studio," says Julien. In this bare-bones room, the album was recorded on a primitive eight-track reel-to-reel tape machine in a week-long burst of chaotic creative energy.

The musicians speak fondly of Draves, whose role as producer was largely to find a framework for the band's musical anarchy. "Dave was a big part of making the record. Maybe, being a bit older, he had some perspective on some of the most ill-advised concepts," Julien laughs. "He was as much part of the band at various times as anyone else, really," says Andrew. "It was because he was so generous with his time and energy that we were able to play with ideas, call our friends [as guest musicians] and pretty much have no limitations in terms of time. You know, when you record in a studio there's a cost dimension that really constrains all that. It really goes back to Dave being generous."

Deflecting praise for the album's special sound, Mike attributes it to "our weird, terrible equipment." Draves backs this up to an extent, discussing the Beillard brothers' gear with a tech geek's genuine bewilderment. "Julien played a Peavey amp. Nobody plays rock with a Peavey amp," he says. As for Mathieu, "he played the most uncool bass of the time, a Yamaha Motion B. I don't know anyone who would walk into a store and buy that, but he didn't give a shit about what anyone else was doing in music."

But of course, it wasn't just the gear. Even from the early recordings, the band's most obvious characteristic sound, the vocal interplay between Mike and Julien, stood out. "The character of it happened naturally, but we had to work really hard to make it sound good," says Mike of their signature harmonizing. "Singing was a challenge for both of them," agrees Draves. "In that sense it was really cool. It was really gawky and nerdy, but completely exciting and powerful."

The vocal coalescence was mirrored by the way the bandleaders' guitars complemented each other. Draves panned the two guitars into the left and right speakers, a technique the band would continue to use on their subsequent recordings. Despite this stereo effect, as a listener I often had trouble distinguishing between the two guitars; they seemed to blend into a seamless whole, sometimes sounding like a lone guitarist playing one incredibly complex part. I always attributed this either to my untrained ear or to my bargain-basement stereo system, so I was relieved to hear that Draves himself heard it the same way. "I'd record them, and I couldn't tell who was playing what," he says. "I've always been a fan of dual guitar players who can weave stuff in and out… they're the masters of that."

Draves had no doubt he was working with a special set of players. "Julien was one of the purest musicians I ever met. It was like you were watching his mind work through the guitar. When he would sit there trying to learn a line, it was like random chaos. It was beautiful to watch."

As for the younger Beillard brother, "he was the oddest guy I'd ever recorded. He didn't really know what he was gonna do, and he just started doing stuff. It was completely improvised and yet really quite compelling. It was like 'what's this guy doing?' He was so exciting to watch." The Beillards's cousin Peter Murray, a trained and professional bassist, agrees. "He didn't have a clue what he was doing, but he was doing all these brilliant things. I'd certainly had a lot more experience, but I'd find myself thinking 'I almost wish that I would think to play stuff like this.'"

Mathieu himself describes his bass style as a bit more thought-out. He'd learned basic technique from a teacher, and as though to confirm Draves's description of the Beillards's jams as "punk jazz," he lists his main influences as Fugazi's Joe Lally and fusion bassists Jaco Pastorius and Stu Hamm (to whom he'd been introduced by his cousin, and who made music, as he describes it, "where the bass was the focal point"). Mathieu is quick to add: "I would say that the strongest influence, though, was the Wooden Stars. The bass lines that I came up with were always dependent on and inspired by the music that the rest of the band was playing, and there was a lot of creative energy there to tap into."

Mathieu took the lead vocal on the album's strangest track, "Hidden Decorations." Over a track whose lurching percussive rhythm and jagged guitars evoke Captain Beefheart (though the band would deny the Captain's influence), Mathieu speak-sings a rambling monologue from the unlikely perspective of a homeless, drunken sailor: *I wander from bar to bar fight, my uniform worn thin, torn threads from violence. My one wooden leg carries a fine leather shoe, I wear it with pride and my happiness is diffused.* As he sings, his voice occasionally cracks; he was only 17.

Though the album's vocals are generally low in the mix, in keeping with the era's self-effacing indie aesthetic, a close listen finds that the band's lyrical approach is strong even at this early stage. At times, the lyrics are what you might expect from a bunch of overly clever teenagers. You've got your one-of-these-things-is-not-like-the-other free association—*Some planets go to bed like virgins* ("The Rocker"), and your absurdly arch vocabulary—*We're all enslaved by our galvanized trenches* ("The Nuclear Warhead"). But even so, the words remain intriguing, mixing grandiose, pseudo-heroic statements with arresting imagery and healthy dollops of humour.

"One thing that's really crucial to understanding the Wooden Stars is that everything was hilarious and serious at the same time," says Mike. "I have a memory of Julien and I [saying] 'Oh shit, we need lyrics for this song.' So I remember one of us lying in a hammock, the other sitting in a lawn chair, and literally passing the notepad back and forth to write the story or whatever of the song, and just cackling and laughing like crazy. Half the things we said were just absurd and got axed, but a lot of things that were also really funny ended up being part of the story that was really sad or touching or whatever."

The album captures a band both innocent and musically ambitious, with horns and reeds (courtesy of local jazzman Peter Kieswalter), a string section and Draves's piano and accordion adding to the already all-over-the-place musical landscape. The band's emerging tendency for commercial self-sabotage can be seen in the album's catchiest tracks being buried in the middle ("Baby Barn," "The Rocker," "Oh! The Agonies of Hell") or at the end ("Innocent Gears") rather than leading off the top.

Some of the songs are also demanding in and of themselves. "Donkeys" features a string arrangement, experimental collage techniques and lyrics that are obscure even by the band's standards (*Nothing murders like a bloodshot donkey* is the decidedly uncatchy chorus). The very next song, the nearly 10-minute "Keith and Amy," begins with a proggy riff, segues into a Pavement-esque verse, drifts into a meandering, seemingly improvised jam, bursts into a hardcore section complete with a larynx-shredding screamed vocal, then circles around to the opening riff again.

The Very Same is long and sprawling at 70 minutes—"that was in the early days of the CD, and the joke was, we were just gonna fill the whole thing," says Draves. It concludes with a seven-minute untitled hidden track (that bastion of the CD era!) consisting mainly of a single chord being repeated at ever-lengthening intervals (word had it that the band members all switched instruments before the very last chord). With toy instruments, stray vocals and what sound like unfinished jams barely audible in the background, the whole track is a microcosm of the album's kitchen-sink approach.

Whether despite or because of all the insanity, the album's mixture of post-punk dissonance, avant-garde rhythms and pure pop songcraft still sounds excitingly original today. "It's a progressive rock album, but as if it were recorded by a high school stage band," laughs Julien. And as scattered and messy as their sound could be, the complex rhythms and riffs showed that there was a tight, well-rehearsed unit at the core. "With music as strange as what we were doing, we had to do it really well—maybe twice as well as your average punk band in order to get the point across," says Mike.

The music is perfectly reflected in the album design. The front cover is an eerie image of a man with a plastic bag on his head riding a donkey. On the back cover is an elaborate collage, and inside are pictures of the extremely youthful band members. All the artwork was by Wyatt Boyd, who says today that his work "now seems a little green"—which is true to some extent, but as such it does fit with the music.

Amid all the busy imagery, the album's name only appears on the disc itself, nor is the label name listed on the sleeve (and, as I've noted earlier, the year of release is nowhere to be found). If you look closely enough, the album was released on Hersenhoren's Lunamoth label. Lunamoth was an indie, but it had major-label distribution in Canada through EMI. The band looked to be on its way.

I saw them live for the first time that summer in Ottawa. It wasn't one of the anarchic shows that their early fans describe. I only have two memories from the show: the chain that Andrew dragged across his snare drum on "Farewell to the Yellow Jacket Avenger," and Julien and Mike's quite uncomfortable stage presence; both of them spent the whole show staring at the floor.

In retrospect it's clear that the Wooden Stars were an acquired taste; even fellow musician Samir Khan, who'd later become a friend and collaborator of the band as well as one of their biggest fans, wasn't impressed the first time he saw them live. "I would say that from your late teens to your early 20s you look to music to confirm your world view, and the Wooden Stars were pretty much the antithesis of that," he says. "They were too dark, too poppy, too weird, too straight... They had these odd, funny-sounding lyrics that had a kind of perversity that you don't really appreciate until you've lived a little."

All the same, I must have liked them enough to keep following them. There was something undeniably intriguing about this band. And they were just getting started.

CHAPTER 3

I'm Not Into Spoonfeeding You The One

"I don't think they meant to be pretentious about it.
The problem is that they were really nerds." –Geoffrey Pye

The Wooden Stars' very first interview was with the *Ottawa Citizen*'s Lynn Saxberg in 1994. I know it was their first because Saxberg makes a point of mentioning it, going on to state that the band is "so green" that they have "no product, no press kit and no hand-out photos." In the article, the 19-year-old Julien is already displaying an ironic wit and self-deprecation, describing their sound as "based on stupid ideas that go too far." Perplexed by the amount of buzz the band had already generated in spite of this low profile, Saxberg asks rhetorically, "What's the deal?"

In her brief piece, Saxberg proceeds to lay the template for everything that would annoy the band about their press coverage through their early career: undue focus on the Sub Pop affair, blithe comparisons of them to the Rheostatics, descriptions of their sound as "quirky" and repeated references to their young age. "The whole reason there was a buzz around us for the first record is because people thought 'They're 18 years old and they're idiot savants!'" says Mike, sounding irritated about it even today.

An interview that Mike and Andrew did with Montreal zine *I Killed Rasputin* (undated, but circa '96 by my research), was typical of their press appearances (most of which have since faded into digital or literal dust; the *Rasputin* interview was reprinted in *Broken Pencil*, where it can still be read online as of this writing). The band members spend the interview stonewalling questions about Sub Pop, firmly denying all the musical influences proposed by the interviewer, and spouting inside jokes. The anonymous writer is left struggling to describe the band, managing only to compare them to a few experimental contemporaries (but, possibly chastened by his sharp-tongued subjects, hastening to add that the Wooden Stars "sound almost nothing like those bands, and are certainly not influenced by them").

Describing the band's sound has vexed many a critic, and no one from their biggest fans to the band members themselves has been able to quite put their finger on it. It was common in the 90s for both critics and indie rock fans to associate them with the nascent "post-rock" movement—if an extraordinarily vague and questionable label used to lump together a bunch of musically disparate bands out of sheer journalistic laziness can be called a movement.

This always annoyed me, partly because the term itself seemed so unbearably pretentious—in its blithe assumption both that rock was over, and that this was what came next—but mainly because I never figured out what the Wooden Stars had in common with the various bands in this nebulous classification. As a young critic in '97, Jonathan Bunce suggested in *Eye Weekly*, cheekily but no doubt accurately, "If these guys were from Chicago or Chapel Hill, they'd be post-rock superstars." Today a veteran Toronto indie music promoter, Bunce says, "I'm surprised at my younger self that I used that genre tag for them. I wouldn't lump them in with that now, and I don't even think that overall they did either."

In retrospect, the band being put in this category makes a bit more sense than I thought at the time. Not being all that meaningful, the term "post-rock" was fluid. Coined by U.K. music critic Simon Reynolds in a 1994 *Mojo* article, who applied it to bands "using rock instrumentation for non-rock purposes," by the late 90s it had come to be associated (at least by critics and the kind of music geek circles I was a part of) with a group of bands from Chicago, mainly associated with labels such as Thrill Jockey, Kranky and Drag City.

Thrill Jockey's most popular act was Tortoise, an instrumental group given to sprawling suites, with whom the Wooden Stars shared a certain musical adventurousness if not a sound per se. I remember thinking that Tortoise-overlapping duo Gastr del Sol sounded at times like an even nerdier version of the Wooden Stars. And the Wooden Stars were known to occasionally play on the same bills as Thrill Jockey bands, from muscular prog punk trio Trans Am to avant pop ensemble The Sea and Cake, no doubt creating an association in the audience's minds.

But my greatest insight into this association didn't come until the writing of this book, when I complained aloud to my wife that I didn't understand it and she replied, with sublime simplicity, "I do. Post-rock is like hipster prog, right?"

Suddenly it was all clear. Prog was so far out of the indie mentality in the 90s that we could have hardly been expected to call a spade a spade. "I never thought of that at the time either," says Julien. "I remember my cousin Peter saying 'Oh, it's like you're trying to be Gentle Giant or something.' I had never heard of that. I thought it was totally bizarre, like 'what?' But it's very prog rock."

Andrew even goes as far as to compare the Wooden Stars to Canadian prog gods Rush (without any prompting from the recovering Rush fan interviewing him). "They're great musicians, but they also write really good songs. I think that's what the Wooden Stars were trying to do," he says.

Indeed, it would seem that the Wooden Stars' use of complicated time signatures is the key to their being called post-rock—or worse still, the even more obnoxious "math rock." Though there's a slight cleverness to the term, equating musical time signatures with mathematical fractions, it seemed to apply more to bands whose songs showed off technical complexity for its own sake—a nerd version of machismo. (Again, I never fully grasped the meaning of the term until recently, when an acquaintance told me, of his time spent in a technical metal band, that he had spent all his time onstage fervently counting). "I always think it's weird that Wooden Stars were lumped in with math rock, and often put on the same bills with math rock bands. I never thought they shared that aesthetic," says Stephen Evans. "The sort of musical acrobatics they did were based on a playfulness and a soulfulness that none of those other bands had."

According to Andrew, this musical complexity was never intended as such, nor did it spring from his theory-trained musical mind. "More often, it came from Mike or Julien's riff that just simply wasn't in 4/4," he laughs. "They couldn't have told you what it was in, but they knew how to play it, and I had to just kind of make it seem together. It wasn't like I was like going 'let's make this complicated.' In fact, I was probably doing the opposite."

But Geoffrey Pye, who was present for several living-room songwriting sessions in the early days, remembers the songs' complexity as a more deliberate choice. "I don't know if they would admit it," he says, "but a lot of the things were puzzles and challenges. I don't think they meant to be pretentious about it. The problem is that they were really nerds, sincerely music nerds," he laughs. "It was very exciting to write something that could be played in 5/8, and then in 7/8, back and forth."

Perhaps the most ridiculous genre the Wooden Stars were assigned was "emo." Here is an interesting fact gleaned from years of informal research: if you ask people what emo means, you will get a different answer 100% of the time. Some years ago when I pressed a friend to define the term, he actually answered "the Wooden Stars." When I later mentioned this to Mike, he nodded sagely and replied, "You know, I've had a lot of opportunity to consider that question, and I've concluded that the answer is: plastic-rimmed glasses and wallet chains."

I always found the term emo particularly meaningless because, at a root level, just about all songwriting has an emotional core. But upon reflection, in a 90s context where most indie rock strove to affect an air of arch, ironic cleverness, the Wooden Stars (though they certainly had a heavy dose of irony in their lyrical arsenal) sang like they meant it, and their audience felt the emotional punch. "They were such a good live band because they were emotional," says Pye, describing their shows as "cathartic" experiences. Mike had a particular skill for capturing a sentiment and getting it across. "When I put the Snailhouse record out," recalls Amy Hersenhoren, "there was some kid who called my office crying because he loved it so much."

The attempts by critics to lump them in with these various genres was of great irritation to the band, who did little to conceal their ire when the topic was brought up in interviews. "Now I look back and I think it's funny, 'cause it seems like a lot of energy to waste on something that doesn't matter that much," says Mike. "If someone's gonna buy the record or come to a show, who cares? They can call it whatever they want. But at the time, I think we were trying to define ourselves, and resisted those kinds of labels."

So if they weren't what people thought, then what genre were they? "That's the problem," Mike laughs. "We were just a bunch of weirdos. We didn't want to go into any genre or anything. There were a few bands that we met over the years that we really identified with, and it was for precisely that reason: when we listened to them, we couldn't figure out what section of the record store they belonged in. For us, that was really attractive. And I think the whole idea of subcultures in music and youth culture was just kind of repugnant to us, for better or for worse," he concludes with a laugh.

Apart from nebulous subgenres, the other easy trick in rock journalism is to make references to other bands. This was another irritant to the Wooden Stars, who often found themselves being compared to bands they hadn't even heard, or to contemporary artists who they might have liked, but didn't consider to be influences.

The go-to reference in the earliest days was the Rheostatics, who I admittedly thought of when I first heard the Wooden Stars. At the time, the Rheostatics were an exciting band; particularly in Canada, it was unusual for a popular band to be so experimental, and vice-versa. The Rheos definitely shared a few common elements with the Wooden Stars: a singer with a trembly falsetto (Martin Tielli), two distinct songwriters whose contrasting styles brought tension and excitement to the sound (Tielli and Dave Bidini) and a drummer with a background in avant-garde music (Dave Clarke). As Draves succinctly puts it, "the Rheostatics were probably the only other band that was doing sort of nerd rock."

But despite these points in common—and the fact that they were indeed Rheos fans (and vice-versa)—the Wooden Stars resented the critical assumption of influence. "It's disappointing when you find someone who you think of as a kindred spirit, and everyone just claims you're ripping them off," says Mike. "But whatever, that happens all the time. That's rock 'n' roll."

By the time their second album *Mardi Gras* came out, casual listeners were more likely to compare the band to Pavement, who at the time were at the top of the indie rock heap. There's definitely a hint of Stephen Malkmus's offhand delivery in Julien's singing voice on the early albums, not to mention a shared lyrical penchant for random imagery, clever humour and obscure references. But Pavement always cultivated a loose approach to their singing and playing; when Malkmus's voice cracked on a high note in the very first line of their song "Silent Kid," it sent a signal, whether unintentionally or by design, that he couldn't be bothered to make the effort. This "slacker" approach, very popular in 90s indie rock, couldn't be further from the Wooden Stars' tight and meticulous songcraft, or their sincere and earnest attitude.

Another point of influence that I and others assumed, evidently incorrectly, was Captain Beefheart. Though the Wooden Stars were never as far out as Beefheart's still unmatchably weird masterpieces *Trout Mask Replica* and *Lick My Decals Off, Baby*, there seemed to be a similarity in the crooked guitar lines and demented lyrical imagery. But Mike decisively dispels the notion. "I had never heard Captain Beefheart at all at that point," he insists. "We ended up enjoying some of it, we used to listen to *Shiny Beast* in the van and stuff, but that was only after people had said that to us, repeatedly, and we became curious." Same goes for the clever English art pop band XTC, discovered by the band only after being compared to them.

Faced with all these denials, I had to break down and ask that lamest of amateur rock-journalist questions: what were their influences? While pointing out that "we were all coming from totally different places," under pressure Mike cops to a few points of reference. "Julien turned me onto a lot of stuff that I knew of, but didn't really know how great it was," he says, mentioning the Clash, the Violent Femmes, Tom Waits and the Replacements. For his part, Julien also cites the Clash, as well as Talking Heads and the Raincoats, as early influences. "But those are pretty standard weirdo rock records," argues Mike. "It's not like we were coming from way underground or anything."

But though the influences themselves may not have been all that obscure, the band devoured musical points of reference and mixed them together in unprecedented ways. "There was a huge catalogue of music that seemed to be required listening material," says Geoffrey Pye, citing "anything from Leonard Cohen to NoMeansNo to James 'Blood' Ullmer and Ornette Coleman" in an average listening session, with the goal of "somehow fusing the most magical parts of these different extreme songwriting styles."

Wyatt Boyd also mentions Ornette Coleman as an influence on the band, in particular Coleman's theory of "harmolodics." David Dacks, a writer and artistic director of Toronto's avant-garde space the Music Gallery, writes on the Weird Canada music blog that harmolodics was "a concept of music with no fixed tonal centre where rhythm, melody and harmony were equally important," which seems to me like a key clue to the band's complex and deliberate approach.

With the benefit of hindsight, the band members can see how their approach may have hindered the way they were perceived. "We set ourselves up to be misinterpreted," admits Mike, while Julien speculates that, "There's something wilfully self-defeating in wanting to subvert what you're doing in a way that almost no one will notice."

All told, I'd have to say my favourite description comes from Josh Latour, who proposes: "Sun Ra had a baby with the Clash. The baby grew up to be an aging man and played on a street corner in New Orleans with his semi-inebriated pals. That is what they sounded like."

CHAPTER 4

Hands to Work

"Given this somewhat odd and somewhat ridiculous sort of aesthetic that we had, that was kind of a high point." –Julien Beillard

I moved from Ottawa to Toronto in 1993 to go to university. By '96, my brother Nick and Mocky had as well. I started spending a lot of time at their place on Manchester Avenue, where they lived with Josh Latour—another Ottawa transplant who'd played with Mocky and Nick since the high school jazz ensemble. I'd spend hours in this environment of pure creativity; sometimes, a collective breakfast prep would turn into a jam session using kitchen implements. Between jams, Mocky would concoct out loud his elaborate and ambitious plans for his musical career. Through these hangouts at the Manchester pad, I would meet Peaches, Gonzales, Feist and Taylor Savvy, a gang of musical friends who would reorient my musical compass once again. But that is a whole other story.

Mocky had a recording studio set up in one of the rooms upstairs, where he would record demos for himself and other people from our overlapping group of musical friends. One day, he played me some new Wooden Stars demos he'd recorded. It sounded different from their earlier stuff, tighter and catchier but somehow even more original. They had taken their sound further.

This material would soon turn up on *Mardi Gras*, their second album. Arguably their finest work, it certainly boasts some of their most classic songs. Even Julien, whose default mode in looking back at the band is harshly self-critical, allows that "given this somewhat odd and somewhat ridiculous sort of aesthetic that we had, that was kind of a high point."

If the band was at the top of their game going in to record *Mardi Gras*, it can be attributed in part to good old-fashioned time spent on the road. Buoyed by Amy Hersenhoren's connections and gifted with a solid work ethic, the band took the opportunity to tour across Canada, with the odd foray into the U.S. Nowadays, as Mike points out, "it's not that weird to get a minivan and cross the country. But in '95, we were really legitimized by our willingness to do that. And it was made easier, because there weren't as many people competing to play at Amigo's in Saskatoon or whatever."

Though things had looked promising for Amy Hersenhoren's label Lunamoth, its corporate parent EMI was unhappy with the label's less than commercial bent. "There were expectations for me to produce less marginal product for them, and I wasn't really interested in doing that," she says. Or as Andrew puts it with characteristic self-deprecation: "When they only sold like 800 copies or whatever, even she couldn't protect us!"

Meanwhile, Mike had slipped an advance copy of the new record to his old friend Julie Doiron. Now broken off from Eric's Trip and making music on her own, she had resurrected her on-again, off-again label, Sappy, with her then husband Jon Claytor. The couple listened to the album in the car during the long drives of a Western Canadian tour. "The more we listened to it, the more we had the songs stuck in our head," she remembers. "We decided we had to put it out."

Right from the album cover, the carnivalesque title in stark contrast to the artwork depicting a bleak Canadian winter landscape, *Mardi Gras* promises and delivers a record full of contrasts and unexpected twists. Julien and Mike's guitar playing has reached a sublime level of musicianship. "At that point, we were learning a lot about music, or so it seemed anyway," says Julien, "and there were a lot of interesting things we discovered about interlocking guitar parts." Andrew's growing role in the band is also prominent; the drums are high in the mix, and the album begins and ends with solo drum beats.

Recorded in 1996 at Toronto's Chemical Sound studio and released the following year, the album finds the band still showcasing a lot of musical ambition. Trumpeter Martin Walters adds his skills to a number of tracks, including a neo-classical horn suite ("The Festival of Fire") and the opening title track, a joyously shambolic take on a jazz parade (also one of the band's weaker tracks; the Wooden Stars were many things, but a New Orleans second line they were not). There's also a quasi-bluegrass number ("The Stolen Banjo") and another sprawling instrumental ("I'm Not Into Spoonfeeding You the One"). But the album's standout songs are upbeat, rollicking tunes that brilliantly synthesize the band's conflicting sensibilities of experimentation and pop catchiness.

After the throwaway opening track fades out, the almost anthemic "Hands to Work" announces the album in earnest. The Beillard brothers' cracking adolescent voices have grown into confident (if still off-kilter) crooning, with Mike's sweet harmonies sprinkled on top. Following a pseudo-proletarian refrain (*Hands to work and hearts to God*) and an absurdist chant (*Revolution! Revolution! Garbage!*), Mathieu sings a chorus whose Yoda-like grammar perfectly complements the melody: *Our visions are yet sleeping, our children will from ashes rise. Long dead and gone, proud lions in their hearts revive. But fear not disenchantment, holy spirits guide our lives.*

"I guess I'm pretty proud of that in a way," says Julien (who showed a tendency in our interview to heavily qualify his statements in this manner) about the song. "The tune had this bizarre sort of chordal and rhythmic density. To us, it felt like this odd, hypnotic but also kind of off-putting feeling. That's the kind of thing that I aspired to at that time, anyway."

On the first album, Julien and Mike's voices were clearly delineated. But on *Mardi Gras*, whether out of deliberate playfulness or just a creative symbiosis, songs would often find Mike affecting a baritone (as in the Chet Baker-esque croon on "Wyatt and Pam in the Botanical Gardens") or Julien singing high harmonies. On some songs, I still can't tell who's singing what.

While the band had got tighter and sharper musically,

they'd also stepped up their lyrical game. If the words on the first album often sound like the inspired and clever, but not particularly profound, work of the talented teenagers that the band were, *Mardi Gras* finds them developed into powerful writers. The album's lyric sheet is full of poetic gems: *The pastures are lonely with the skeletons of birds* ("The Sparrows, the Grackles, the Emus") and startling imagery: *A baby was trampled by the jubilant throngs. Now it lies in the garbage, underneath a flower stall* ("The Gravenhurst Militia").

"The Cigarette Girl" is another album highlight. A catchy riff in a relatively straightforward 6/8 time leads into lyrics combining rock n' roll clichés (*Met her at the high school dance*), inside jokes (*And there's nothing in this metropolis but the sound of stolen banjos*), old-timey slang (*Grandpa said she was just another pool hall hussy*) and an ephemeral but catchy chorus (*She's a good cigarette, the kind that makes you forget*). Then the song takes a swerve into another key, and Julien sings a disarmingly frank expression of nerdy alienation: *That's me, conductor of stilted conversations, the university, some kind of scent of perspiration, that's me*, before the song lurches back into the main riff.

This mashing together of various voices and emotions is destabilizing, with the tone constantly changing from violent to goofy, personal to obscure and back again, united by a high-flown, bombastic spirit that both was and wasn't ironic. "The sort of ridiculous grandiosity of our songs was always tongue-in-cheek," says Mike. "Musically, we were really big and brash, and we always had these sort of idealistic characters in the songs. I think you could run with it as some sort of really serious commentary on something, and it was, but we also laughed at the idea that you could say anything effective through a rock song. Those two ideas in opposition is what's magical to me when I look back on it. I know when we were being ridiculous, and it was most of the time," he laughs. "But I also know that we were being really genuine and earnest."

Like a lot of great songwriting duos, Julien and Mike represented polarities of dark in light, as much in their individual personalities as their music. Mike was always friendly and warm; Julien, hyper-intelligent and caustic; where they overlapped, other than musically, was in a shared sense of humour. Well known to their friends, this comedic connection contrasted with the serious image they projected in the media. "What we would have said at the time," Julien says, "is that we were serious about the music that we were making, but that we also had some kind of detachment from that whole activity and could have a laugh about that too. It's a pompous, self-flattering way of putting it. But we actually were just really goofy. We were maybe less serious than just socially inept."

Mathieu remains the band's secret weapon on *Mardi Gras*, singing lead on the album's closer and possibly the band's single best song, "Country Violins." The song jumps straight into what at first threatens to resemble a straight-forward country pop riff, before an almost Zeppelin-esque cascade of crashing chords and cymbals sets it careening in another direction. This twisted take on country is reflected in Mathieu's lyrics, a delirious dark fantasy of rural life that still, whether heard or read, gives me shivers to this day:

I'm winding him up and dance to the country violins.
There's a warning in fat and toothless parting grin,
insects boiling over in his pants, hay in his hair. I've
never been all there upstairs, in the loft, my daddy
is grunting like a pig. And the worms inside me toss
and bind away, weaving death shrouds and mourn-
ing veils for us country boys from death to the womb,
gifted with nature and living backwards... And I feel
for the lambs with their throats slit, bloody necklace
drooling wine from a gurgling line in one day like
fly-tape... and it's out of my hands... country violins.
(...) In the heat and haze, opiates flood his face, and
the phonograph is scratching. Daylight is dangerous,
I save it in a deerskin flask when it drips from cows'
tongues licked through the barn wall cracks. I drink
it and dream of rivers steaming and green, every
stump bleeding in the forest where venison urine
creeps... And I feel for the lambs with their throats
slit, dark red sun drips through fleece and warm
breath in one day like fly-tape... and it's out of my
hands... country violins.

When asked to describe the inspiration for this brilliant lyricism, Mathieu's response is as prosaic as his song's imagery is
unhinged. "We had written the music for the song first. Julien
suggested to me that I should write the lyrics. I found that the
verse had a sort of country feel to it, so I wanted to write lyrics
that had a rural setting. As for the theme and storyline, they
just sort of gradually developed from a smattering of images
and plays on words that I liked and pieced together."

Though he was responsible for this high point in the band's discography, Mathieu was disillusioned. Just as the album was released, and shortly before the band left on tour to promote it, he quit.

The other band members suggest various reasons for this dramatic departure. "I think he just didn't really enjoy the life of sleeping on floors," says Mike. "When we would go to Toronto for the weekend or wherever the hell it was, when we were going out to a bar or restaurant and hanging out with people, all the things you have to enjoy to be a rock band, he wasn't enjoying any of that. Neither were the rest of us, really, but we had more of a tolerance for it than he did."

Also, as Andrew points out, Mathieu was "a high school student, trying to get good enough grades so he could go to university, and we were trying to drag him out of class to drive off to Winnipeg to do a show or whatever!" Julien, for his part, declined to speculate on the reasons for his brother leaving the band: "To this day, I don't really know. Maybe I just won't comment on that."

But when I was finally able to contact Mathieu himself by email, he was straightforward about his reasons. "I was feeling generally restless," he writes. "I went through a stretch where I was dissatisfied with my bass playing, in part because I had very little training or knowledge of music theory. I probably also felt that I should focus on my schooling as I was getting a bit older by that time.

"I regret my decision now," he adds with disarming candour. "I probably could have balanced both going to school and playing music, but at the time it seemed like the right decision to me."

Mathieu's sudden departure was unexpected and, as the band members' differing perspectives indicate, unexplained. "He wasn't that communicative," says Mike. "None of us were; we were just cracking jokes all the time and sometimes lashing out at each other, but we weren't actually talking about much. So when he quit, it was a bit of a shock to all of us."

With the tour coming up to support *Mardi Gras*, the band had to find a replacement fast. Luckily they had someone close by: Josh Latour, who'd moved back to Ottawa. Though he was an old friend of my brother's, I didn't know Josh well, but he always struck me as easy-going, funny, eccentric and extremely musical. When I heard he'd joined the band, it seemed to make sense.

It's a little-known chapter in the Wooden Stars' history that they had in fact begun to play as a five-piece just before Mathieu quit, with Josh on keyboards, his first instrument. According to Josh, this version of the band only performed a single show. (In the end, the short lifespan of the five-piece line-up may have been a blessing; a friend of mine who saw the show said that it bordered on "outright fusion.")

Given Josh's natural musical abilities, the other members figured he could simply move over to fill the vacant slot on bass. As Josh remembers it, the transition happened immediately. "I had all my keyboards set up at the practice and we were getting going when Mathieu announced he was leaving the band," he recalls. "Right then and there I became the bass player. The only hiccup was I didn't own a bass, nor had I ever played the bass before. Mathieu sold me his gear, I learned to play as best I could, and we were touring within months."

I suggested to Andrew that it must have altered the

band's musical dynamic to have another jazzbo in the fold. "Except that we put him on an instrument that he didn't know how to play," he laughs. "Even though he was the only one who could read music and talk about theory, it was of limited value." But though he may have been learning his instrument on the fly, there's no denying that Josh's musical sensibility, as Julien puts it, "certainly changed the band in a really radical way."

Mathieu's bass playing, whether intentionally or not, was avant-garde, creating a push-and-pull with Andrew that contributed to the messy energy of the band's early sound. "He and Andy always had a bit of a conflict," says Julien. "It's hard to conciliate when it's the rhythm section who are at odds. For it to work, they both have exactly the same degree of laxness or something. I feel like at first Mathieu was a bit frustrated, because he felt like 'this is just not drumming!' But later, Andy decided that he wanted to play more of that conventional role of a drummer, and was really frustrated by Mathieu's bass playing because it was so all over the place!" he laughs.

Josh, by contrast, brought a solid musical bedrock to the band, a quality that would make their sound from here on out a lot less chaotic. He may not have been trained on the bass, but in addition to his musical training he had an innate sense of rhythm. It brought the band's musicality up a notch, and even Mathieu says that "I like the albums I played on, but I like the subsequent ones as much if not more."

But before he could contribute to the band's sound, Josh first had to learn his way. According to Andrew, "Josh spent a lot of time trying to figure out what the hell [Julien and Mike] were doing, and how it would fit into a context that made sense from a pure theory perspective. I think nine times out of ten, it didn't really. He just knew all the rules were being broken."

I saw the Wooden Stars live for the second time that summer. The difference a few years in the game had made was immediately visible. Where Mike and Julien had stared at the floor the whole first show I'd seen, this time their eyes were wide open, staring confidently to the back of the room. The *Mardi Gras* songs sounded great, and the rhythm section had a new solidity. The club was full of people, and the band seemed to be on their way up. But typically, their next move would be a sideways detour.

CHAPTER 5

Romantic Machinery

"In Ottawa, anyone who is a half-decent person and a half-decent musician ends up knowing each other eventually." –Samir Khan

During the late 90s, I didn't get back to Ottawa much. I was busy living in Toronto, finishing school, getting married, starting my writing career and making my own music. Meanwhile, after years of being the perpetual outsiders of the Ottawa scene, the Wooden Stars found themselves at the centre of a developing musical community.

Various members of the band played at different times with Samir Khan's band Kepler and Geoffrey Pye's Yellow Jacket Avenger. Andrew played drums with Clark, led by John Tielli (younger brother of the Rheostatics' Martin). Both Mike and Andrew played with singer-songwriter Jim Bryson. There was also a little-known project called The Killers featuring Pye, Tim Kingsbury and Julien on drums. (Needless to say, the band was unrelated to the corporate-alternative juggernaut of the same name that surfaced a few years later, although Kingsbury relates that "I told the guys in The Killers that we had a band called The Killers." He deadpans: "They didn't react.")

And of course, throughout the Wooden Stars' entire existence, Mike's project Snailhouse was on a parallel track, releasing an impressive six albums and two EPs between 1994 and 2011 (after which Mike dropped the Snailhouse moniker to perform under his own name). There was considerable overlap with the Wooden Stars—Andrew, Julien and Josh all play on Snailhouse's 1998 album *The Radio Dances*, with Andrew on nearly every song—but there's no confusing the two bands. Snailhouse is a project worthy of its own separate focus, but it's fascinating to listen to as a Wooden Stars fan for the way it illustrates the evolution of Mike's songwriting sensibility, what he brought to the band and how different he sounded without it.

"I think I had a bit of tension around that," says Mike of balancing the two projects. "Sometimes I would hoard things that maybe would have been better Wooden Stars songs, and other times maybe I tried to force songs into the Wooden Stars that would have been better treated separately. But generally, anything that was really quiet or really personal ended up as a Snailhouse song." Displaying Mike's gifts for melody and lyricism, Snailhouse's music also shows that his deep songwriting and complex guitar skills can stand on their own. The project was also a kind of hub for the Ottawa music community, with Khan, Doug Tielli (another member of the Tielli musical dynasty) and future Arcade Fire members Kingsbury, Jeremy Gara and Richard Parry all contributing to Snailhouse recordings and performances.

This Ottawa "scene" (whose veterans invariably bristle at the term, insisting that it was more of a small group of friends—though I'd argue that most "music scenes" are similar, at least in origin) developed naturally. "In Ottawa, anyone who is a half-decent person and a half-decent musician ends up knowing each other eventually," says Khan by way of explanation. "I have no idea why [the Wooden Stars] took us on as little brothers—at the time the bands I played in were okay, but not in the same class. Maybe they saw something, or maybe they were just tired of being lonely."

This kind of self-deprecation was a recurring theme in my conversations with the Wooden Stars and their collaborators, to the point where I started to wonder if this was an ingrained part of the Ottawa psyche. "It can't seem to produce anything that it feels comfortable being proud of. It's so tentative," complains Pye of his hometown. "It has a very strange sense of questioning oneself, that I think was a common thread throughout all the bands that were part of that scene. They came from a very staunch background, strict parents who worked for the government and decided that things like music were a waste of time."

And yet, parental disapproval of rock music is hardly a site-specific phenomenon. In fact, you could even say it's served as fuel for generations of musicians. But there's something to Pye's thesis about a local habit of chronic self-doubt and self-questioning, at least if the Ottawa artists I know are any indication.

"Ottawa simply doesn't give a shit about so many things," says Wyatt Boyd. "I remember one day Michael Jackson was walking around downtown—something to do with his involvement in *Miss Cast Away* " (one of MJ's doomed movie projects, shot in the capital city). "His sudden appearance failed to cause even so much as a stir—everyone just went out about their usual business. Which in a way is great; it's one of the things I've always appreciated about the city: the near-perfect anonymity that almost any one can have here. But at the root of it all is a peculiar type of apathy which is not particularly healthy, especially if you're trying to build up a following here. For years the band would play shows that could easily have been their debut appearance, with zero guarantee as to who would be there: sometimes a full house, sometimes not enough people to even merit their beer tickets."

The city is at a distinct disadvantage for the kind of culture that fuels creativity. With approximately an eighth of the population working for the government and almost as great a number working in the high-tech industry, it's a mecca for people who could be called, for lack of a better word, square (or if you were feeling even less generous, boring).

And unlike a city like, say, Winnipeg or Edmonton, forced by geographical isolation to develop its own culture, Ottawa is so close to Toronto and Montreal that most creatively minded people eventually move to one of those cities, if not beyond. Perhaps because so many of its young, creative people end up either moving away or shackling on the "golden handcuffs" of a government job, artistic movements in the city tend to come and go in waves. Depending on your perspective, the Wooden Stars' heyday was one of these waves, or just happened to fall in between them.

All the same, being in Ottawa wasn't entirely negative

for the band or their community. "It was just the right size that everybody supported each other," says Gara, who has a more cheerful take on the capital city than many of his fellow veterans. "It wasn't big enough that you could make a mark, so you were only doing it if you really wanted to."

And the community around the band was also characterized by a trait that I always think of as quintessentially Ottawa, a penchant for elaborate joking. "The glue in that whole scene was humour," says Stephen Evans. "Everybody had a really dark, playful and twisted sense of humour. All my best memories of the Wooden Stars are of going in the van with them to whatever city and just pissing myself. Julien and Mike would go on these rolls." Kingsbury has similar memories, recalling that the songwriters' penchant for creating absurd characters also took place on a social level. "They would just go on for an hour on one character. That was one thing I really loved about hanging out with those guys. You'd get sucked into this world that didn't exist, to the point where you felt nauseous from laughing."

On occasion, this sense of humour would spill into their performances. "I remember seeing them in Sackville at this weird show," says Gara. "There was bad weather, so the promoters said it was cancelled, but it wasn't. So there were like 20 people who stuck it out in this big church. Mid-set, Mikey put down his guitar and curled up in a ball in the kick drum as Julien narrated the birth of Jesus. They kind of acted it out as Andy was still playing drums." He adds almost redundantly: "They could be out there at times."

The band's touring during this period resulted in one of the funniest, darkest road stories I've ever heard. Playing at an empty club in the U.S. Midwest, too broke for a hotel room and without any audience members to crash with, the band ended up sleeping on the floor of the club. (When I prodded Josh for the story with this detail, he said "that actually happened a few times, so you'll have to be more specific.") On a quest for more comfortable sleeping arrangements, an inebriated Josh stumbled through the darkened building and eventually found a couch to crash out on. When he awoke the next morning, he slowly realized that the couch had no cushions, that it was in the basement of a derelict building next door to the club, and that he was surrounded by homeless people who'd also found the basement suited their needs.

The period between *Mardi Gras* in '97 and the Wooden Stars' next album two years later was creatively fruitful. Aside from frequent touring, this period saw the release of not only Snailhouse's *The Radio Dances* but the Wooden Stars' little-known *Rise Up and Get Down*. This vinyl-only rarity, released by Ontario-based hardcore/emo label Rhythm of Sickness, served as a kind of "greatest hits" album, with four songs from *The Very Same*, three from *Mardi Gras*, a number never released elsewhere called "Night-Time" and what Mike calls a "Josh-ified remix" of *The Very Same* epic "Keith and Amy."

In the midst of all this creative activity, the band lost a key ally in the music industry when Amy Hersenhoren put her Canadian projects on hold and moved to New York, where she started an experimental music label called Bingo with musician (and future *New Yorker* music critic) Sasha Frere-Jones. The Wooden Stars would be self-managed from here on out, with Andrew taking on the role of de facto manager.

Mike remembers that at the beginning of the band's career, Andrew had "a gigger kind of mentality. Like, he'd jam with us and then go do some jazz gigs, and he'd bring his own car to the gigs. We had come from this kind of punk rock world, where we sort of shared all the shitty work together. He was kind of doing his own thing. He'd just show up and play drums really amazingly, and then we'd kind of go our separate ways."

But when the need to self-manage arose, "he really took the reins, and he basically started effectively managing our inner workings, and communicating with the outside world. He brought a certain amount of ambition to it, and a certain amount of savvy. He knew to ask for more and to push for more, and get better things. I admired that, because I don't think I ever would have clued in that we could make things better for ourselves," Mike laughs.

"For better or worse, I certainly was the one who initiated all the grant writing and tried to coordinate tours, all those managerial tasks. But I didn't really know what I was doing," says Andrew with his customary self-deprecation. "Someone had to do it. Julien wasn't really the guy, Josh definitely wasn't the guy. I'm sure Mike could have done it, but I was probably a little pushier and more Type A than anyone else, just trying to cram a round peg through a square hole and get something happening."

And something needed to happen. Though all the members had day jobs, the band required a lot of time and effort to sustain. In the meantime, they'd lost another label when Julie Doiron and Jon Claytor's on-again, off-again Sappy

Records went, well, off again. "Neither of us were business-people," explains Doiron. With *Mardi Gras* having sold out its limited run, "we weren't in a position to repress it, so the rights just kind of went back to them." But her collaboration with the band was about to get even deeper.

Although she was an old friend of Mike's, not to mention the band's label head for *Mardi Gras*, on paper Julie Doiron seems like an odd match with the Wooden Stars. Musically, her songs are as sparse as theirs are busy; lyrically, she's as bluntly personal as they are abstruse. Their stage patter consisted largely of obscure inside jokes, alternately dark and goofy, while she was notorious for apologizing between songs. And yet, just as the band were hitting their creative and commercial peak, they took on a gig as Doiron's backing band.

Having split up with Eric's Trip in 1996, Doiron was preparing to release her second solo album, *Loneliest in the Morning*, on Sub Pop the following year. "My Sub Pop rep knew who they were and knew I was friends with them," Doiron recalls. "She was like 'why don't you get the Wooden Stars guys to be your band when the record comes out?' It was a pretty quiet record, so it seemed like a pretty crazy idea." Adds the self-deprecating singer: "I just thought they wouldn't be interested."

Nonetheless, she approached the topic with Mike in Winnipeg, at the end of a Sappy Records tour featuring both acts. Well reputed as a team player always game for a collaboration, he agreed to participate and said he'd bring it up with the band. The long drive back to Ottawa gave the guys ample opportunity for discussion. When they got back home, Doiron received a phone message confirming that the Wooden Stars were on board.

"I didn't know everyone would wanna do that, but everyone jumped at it," recalls Mike. Says Andrew, "I remember encouraging us to do it, because I was pretty desperate to be busy and to play music. If that was the opportunity in front of us, I thought we should take it. I knew it would be a possibly interesting clash of her songwriting with our rather strange perspective on what a backing band should do."

Doiron took the band on a three-month tour of the U.S. and Canada, with the Wooden Stars both backing her up and doing their own opening set. In contrast to Andrew's self-description, she remembers that "they were awesome as a backing band. They were great at listening, picking up off each other and improvising."

"I think it was a surprise how fun it was, and easy-going," says Mike. "We actually got along really great, and I think we all enjoyed the music." Over the following few years, the Wooden Stars continued to perform with Doiron in between their musical and other obligations, becoming closely intertwined both musically and personally. "Julie really seems like a sister to me in a lot of ways," says Josh today. Eventually, as Mike recalls, they thought the collaboration should be commemorated. "We were doing all that touring, all this work, and we thought 'Oh, it'd be really nice if we could record like this.'"

Over the 1998-99 Christmas holidays, the band joined Doiron in Fredericton, New Brunswick to record an album together. "Fredericton was like a ghost town, there was literally no one in the entire town," says Andrew. "And we were just sort of seconded in this weird motel, recording this record on the fringes of town with this weird dude, I can't even remember his name." That would be Lloyd Hanson, "who'd been hired to engineer (or produce, depending on who you ask)," as Mike writes in the entertaining Wooden Stars discography on his website.

The distinction between the roles of engineer and producer is a fine one, that can be defined many ways but that fundamentally comes down to who's in charge. "We weren't really producible," Andrew admits. "There's a lot of strong heads in the band. Myself, Julien for sure, and Mike to some degree as well. We were pretty stubborn guys, and we weren't interested in being told how to do things. And I think he thought he was very much the producer of the album, but we never saw it like that." All the same, Andrew admits that the whole experience "was sort of fun in the way that it was like going to rock camp."

The album, which both is and isn't a Wooden Stars record, is a fascinating entry in their discography. Though Mike and Julien's guitar interplay is as intricate as ever, and the rhythm section makes a lot of creative choices, it's intriguing to see the band holding back as much as they do. The true test of a band's virtuosity is its ability to play *less*—Rush, to return to the ultimate prog example, seem constitutionally incapable of running through four bars without some kind of showoffy flourish—and this album shows the Wooden Stars more than capable of taming their impulse towards busy complexity.

On closing track "Sweeter," we hear the Wooden Stars'

voices at the fore for the first time on the album. It's a beauti-fully simple duet with Julien; Mike joins in on harmonies for a dramatic closing chorus. Again, it's almost jarring to hear such emotionally plain-spoken and direct lyrics (*I wonder, was it something I said? What can I do to make this change?*) from the same mouths that have brought us all these puzzles and abstract poetry. The seemingly counterintuitive pairing, with the Wooden Stars' energy and subversive sense of fun contrasting Doiron's minimal song forms and unrelentingly melancholy tone, actually brings out the best in both.

CHAPTER 6

Rebel Radios

"It's sort of a Flaubert novel of an album." –Alex Frenette

In March 1999, only a few months after completing the album with Doiron, the Wooden Stars were back in the studio to record their third album. This time around, they reunited with Dave Draves, who in the interim had improved his studio setup after visiting the *Mardi Gras* sessions in Toronto. "I saw the process, and at that point I brought my studio up a serious notch," he recalls. "There was a real parallel between what they were doing and what my studio was doing," he adds, in the sense that "the first time was pure naïveté." But five years after *The Very Same*, "it was a critical move for those guys to make a great album."

The Moon finds the band having tamed the chaotic energy of their first two albums, instead exploring simpler and more straightforward song forms. No doubt Josh's thoughtful musicianship was one reason; the band's experience as a restrained backing band for Doiron was probably another. But according to Andrew, there was also a deliberate effort to make their sound more accessible.

"I think I was probably pushing it in that direction," he says. "We came out of the gates swinging with a really experimental concept, and then over time that sort of got abandoned or watered-down." Though he'd started off as the band's resident free-jazzer, refusing on principle to play straight rock beats, Andrew's perspective eventually swung in the other direction. In a 2005 interview with the *Ottawa Citizen*'s Fateema Sayani, Andrew went so far as to call the band's first record "completely unlistenable" and state that the band was no longer "trying to impress anyone with stupid musician wankiness like writing songs with two people playing in different time signatures or with harmonies that are the most complicated thing since Schoenberg, and trying to pack it all into a pop song."

In our interview, Andrew was candid that the reasons behind his change of heart were as much commercial as artistic. "To be honest, I think you have to be a very strong personality and really be passionate about playing experimental music to carry on doing it year after year after year, 'cause what it means is that you're gonna have a lot of shows where there's no one there, and a lot of shows where you're literally playing for free or worse. I think I, to be honest, didn't have the self-confidence or the stomach for it. I was hungrier to have things go a little more mainstream in the hopes that that would make it easier and have something make sense financially. I knew it wasn't gonna last if we couldn't figure out a way to make it pay the bills."

In a way, it's funny to think of *The Moon* as pop or commercial effort. It's very much still a Wooden Stars album;

what they may have considered "mainstream" is still far left afield of how most people would define the term. All the same, it's definitely interesting as a listener to hear them streamline and trim the fat from their sound, resulting in a record that spotlights their pop side more than any other in their discography. No one would confuse this with post-rock. (In fact, the band may have doubly cursed themselves with the pop effort; some casual listeners who liked the experimental elements of the early records didn't find *The Moon* to their taste). At only 33 minutes, it's also a concise document of where the band was musically.

Julien is harsh in his judgement of *The Moon*. "By the time we made that record, we were 25 and not 19," he laughs, "and more respectful of hallowed traditional forms of rock music and songwriting. But we were too conservative. If maybe the songs are a bit better, then they should have been presented in a freer spirit. We put so much work into that third record, and I think it sounds very sterile and tame and boring."

But Julien overstates the case; while the anarchic spirit of the first two records has certainly dissipated, *The Moon* finds the band at the top of their game both musically and lyrically, and the album has some of their best songs. What you do notice on a closer listen is a division in the songwriting; for the first time, you can clearly hear which songs are Mike's and which are Julien's. "I think that's just literally what was happening to us," says Mike. "We weren't as intertwined as we had been, emotionally and in terms of actually spending time together."

Though the band members step around the subject, undoubtedly wary of opening old wounds, it's clear that the recording was a difficult one for the band. Josh alludes to "some drama with Julie," but the rest of the band, as well as their colleagues, remain tight-lipped on the details of the strife. "There was definitely conflict around the end of *The Moon*," says Draves. "Just to be frank, the relationships were coming unhinged."

Part of it had to do with the tension between the two song-writers, in particular Julien's increasing unhappiness with the band's career and his resulting mood swings. "Julien is a real presence, and when he's dictating what's going on, it can be great if he's in a good mood, or it can be a total failure," says Draves. "He wasn't clear and direct musically with the guys at all; he was really hard to work with at that point. Josh and Andrew always highly respected him, so it was never a question of calling a spade a spade. But Mike just didn't need that. Mike's a great sport, but he would never say it was easy. A lot of the music came out of real conflict."

Mike agrees that it was a difficult time for the band, but ever the diplomat, he simply says that "we had spent almost a decade together trying to do something collaborative, and that's just really hard for any combination of people."

The division between the two songwriters is made starker by the fact that on the opening two tracks, Mike's "Outlaws" and Julien's "Rebel Radios," the band's trademark harmo-nies are sung by Julie Doiron instead of the familiar vocal duo. (As a side note, Kathleen Edwards, who would later become an acclaimed singer-songwriter in her own right, plays violin on both songs).

But though the two were writing separately, their mutual influence could still be heard. "Julien's songs got more beautiful from Mike's influence in a subtle way, although I don't know if Julien would ever say that," says Draves, while Stephen Evans suggests that Julien's influence pushed Mike's lyrics into darker territory. At any rate, the album's lyrics are stronger than ever, more focused and with a generally more sombre and melancholy tone than before. And for the first time, some of the songs have (relatively) clear overarching storylines.

The soft and understated "Outlaws," a typically unorthodox choice for an opener, is sung from the unusual point of view of someone watching a movie about themselves. *In the film they made us a little more articulate, a little less afraid or something, with a lot more attitude and grace... And we danced like we never really could dance in a scene designed to make you think of the old days.* Veering slightly off topic, the song concludes with some of Mike's loveliest lyrical imagery: *And we lose soft consonants, the boom disturbed by every coastal breeze. You lean in close—"Of course I love you"—an empty screen a blank apparition—and we can't even really say goodbye here 'cause everyone will move in a little closer.*

Julien's "Poison Glass" is another narrative song, set in the midst of some unidentified urban guerrilla warfare. *When the grenadiers were lost in the vineyard, the moon was silver and full and showed us their trail. We surrounded their convoy and lit our fuses. We smoked them out confused, terrified and glassy-eyed. They never had a chance to say goodbye and some of them cried.* Although the song's references to archaic military terms (*Cattle cars and bayonets will sleep in our beds*) seem to indicate that it takes place in the past, the recent wars in Bosnia and Rwanda no doubt informed this pre-War on Terror setting. Ranging from poetic (*Often we wake to find our tears have turned to wine; The bomb squad woke from a dream of a planet without fire*) to jarringly violent (*When I kiss a dusty floor that tastes like a bandage, I think of all the oaths and vows that break with my tongue. I think of you sometimes, your eyes avoiding mine, as you were suspended from a tree*), the lyrics brilliantly evoke this half-told story.

Some of the lyrics hint at the band's growing frustration with the grind of touring and the music business in general. From Mike's "The Summer I Drank Myself to Death": *I hate the night-life—the crowds and the headlights—I laugh when the dancing girls go by (...) Rock 'n' roll will never heal unless you feed it*. From Julien's "Rebel Radios": *Under quarantine of the rock 'n' roll industries (...) I never had a peaceful night 'cause they play the hits all night, and you'll need an alibi. You could say you were left of the dial*.

The album's closer, "Baby, You've Got What I Need," co-written by Julien and Geoffrey Pye, starts off marrying a typically clever twist on the everyday (*Shades shudder with the breeze. I stir in this replica of sleep*) to a rock 'n' roll cliché (*Baby you've got what I need. You're the bird and I'm the bee*). The lyrics go on to drop what reads like a hint at the band's frayed songwriting partnership (*Impossible to please, we both tried our best to come clean. Two hearts that never speak. We just agree on a beat worth keeping*). After some more beautifully abstract poetry (*Demons and lakes and mountains and orchards are pressed like flowers between the pages*), the song concludes with some lovely *sha-na-nas*, as though words have failed.

While still working to complete the album, the once again

label-less band was approached by Matlock, a small indie based in Ste-Foy, a suburb of Quebec City. The label had been started in 1997 as a one-man operation by young Alex Frenette, later expanded to a small three-man team with his twin brother Nick and their Sackville, New Brunswick-based partner Dennis Amos. The label was put on the map (in the small world of Canadian indies) with the success of Halifax indie rockers North of America.

After this, recalls Frenette, "We were just thinking of 'what band would we like on our label?,' just a pie-in-the-sky wish list." The Wooden Stars topped that list: "I felt it would fit with the general aesthetic and the general scene we were trying to document." This scene, which Frenette struggles to define, was often described as "math rock" at the time. "I'm not sure if I ever completely got that, but a lot of our releases tended to be influenced by a slightly sophisticated sense of rhythm," Frenette says. The Wooden Stars' music, he adds, "was complex, yet very memorable. They were one of the most interesting, challenging and also rewarding bands out there." He "almost randomly reached out" to Andrew, then took a bus to Ottawa to meet the band in person at one of their shows.

Impressed with Frenette's initiative, the band started talks for Matlock to release their next album, which was already almost complete. The label was small, but extremely enthusiastic. "The Wooden Stars were pretty much my favourite band on the planet," recalls Amos, "and the possibility and anticipation of putting out a record for them was incredibly motivating."

Matlock released the album in mid-1999, putting all their efforts into promoting it. It went straight to the top of the

Canadian college charts, and with the label exceptionally hiring a U.S. radio promotions firm, it even cracked the American Top 200. Critics were thrilled. "The best band in Canada?" suggested their critical champion Jonathan Bunce in Toronto's *Eye Weekly*, his question mark softening the praise with classic Canadian timidity, before concluding: "No one else dares go so far."

Still, Matlock remained a bedroom operation. "They probably would have done more and better things if they were with a bigger label that had more resources," Frenette admits. "Instead, they had three incredibly passionate 20-year-olds working their asses off for them, but I'm not sure that compares to what a larger label could have done for them." Frenette still feels that the album holds up better than a lot of work from the band's contemporaries. "It's sort of a Flaubert novel of an album," he laughs.

On a strictly aesthetic note, the album's cover displayed the short-term thinking that characterized the era's approach to packaging in the music business both mainstream and indie. (A few years later, with the downloading era in full swing and CD sales in free fall, record cover design experienced a renaissance, as the need to give physical albums an object value became an acute concern). Whereas the first two Wooden Stars records had intriguing cover art, *The Moon*'s CD cover is a photo of the band, in soft focus and so dimly lit as to be barely visible. The graphic design, with its dated 90s digital fonts, feels like a bit of an afterthought.

The band put aside their differences enough to hit the road once again to support *The Moon*. With the years of touring under their belt, they were still a great live band, and a show they played that fall at the Halifax Pop Explosion stands out to some of their fans as their best ever. Samir Khan, who played the same festival with Kepler, recalls: "*The Moon* had come out and it was considered by Wooden Stars fans to be their 'pop' record. People who knew them loved it, but I think they missed some of the loosey-goosey experimentalism of their first few records. That show they put two and two together. They had been on tour for a long time, and were probably at their height of popularity and they were in total control. Songs would fly apart into weird sections and then come back to these strange magical hooks. The crowd, which was pretty substantial, ate it up."

But the heavy touring load was starting to strain on the band; as Draves succinctly puts it, "they got tired of smelling each other in the van." Back at home, they played another show that their friends remember as a low point. "There were some very obvious personal strains that were beginning to show their roots to people who know them," says Khan. During that show at the Downstairs Club, one of the same small venues they'd been playing since the early days, Julien became visibly upset and ended up walking off the stage.

"I think the rest of the band was kind of annoyed with it, but I thought it was part of the performance and took it as that," says Pye. Other friends were taken aback. "It was still a great show by most people's standards, but it was heartbreaking—and more than a bit rattling—to watch," says Khan. "If I really reflect on it, it was one of those times that you realize that failure, despite an enormous amount of talent, is a very real and viable option."

CHAPTER 7

Poison Glass

"Some people decide they're okay with slugging it out and some people don't." –Julie Doiron

The Wooden Stars began the new millennium, as it was excitedly called at the time, with one of their strangest shows ever. In their capacity as Julie Doiron's band, they were invited to open for the Tragically Hip at Toronto's Air Canada Centre on New Year's Eve 1999-2000.

At the time, the gig seemed huge—opening for Canada's biggest band on what seemed (a bit absurdly, in retrospect) to be a significant historical moment—but the reality was unglamorous. "We played at like 7 p.m.; the place wasn't even a quarter full at that point," recalls Mike. "And it was really weird, 'cause the PA was at the other end of the stadium, so every time we played a note there would be like a one-second delay before it came out of the mains. It was insane. And playing that kind of subtle music in that environment was... musically, it wasn't that fun, but it was a really cool opportunity."

The Hip also took the band as openers on a brief jaunt to the U.S. With Andrew unable to join this leg, Josh moved to the drums, with Dave Draves sitting in on bass. Mike remembers the experience as great, though Josh compares opening for the Hip to "looking into a candy store from outside the window." But after two and a half years, the Doiron project had run its course, although Mike admits that "we did it kind of backwards;" the album was the culmination of their collaborative work rather than a fresh project they could develop and promote.

Back in Ottawa, the Wooden Stars as a band proper was running out of steam. "We just literally couldn't finish a song," says Andrew. "We'd create the bedrock for a verse and the bedrock for a chorus, but we wouldn't have a melody or lyrics. We'd end up after three, four, five months of trying half-heartedly with three or four unfinished segments that no one in particular was able to kick over the finish line. It was just really obviously creatively expired."

Andrew attributes this stagnation to the band's laborious songwriting process, depending as it did on long collaborative jams. "It works really well when you're 19 and have endless amounts of free time to practice three or four times a week and drink beer and just have fun, but when you've only got a couple hours a week and you've got all these other things in your life distracting you... that's a very time-consuming way to write music. Unless you have 15 hours a week to throw at it collectively, it just doesn't work."

And all the members had their preoccupations outside the band. Mike was continuing to tour and record as Snail-house, Julien was completing his master's in philosophy, and

Andrew had started to work in Ottawa's high-tech sector. "It was very normal life stuff that got in the way," he explains. "If a band can't get to the point where it's helping you survive, then it is truly a hobby or a labour of love. You can't just do that, so you have to find something else to do. Everyone found other shit to do, which is only natural."

But there were deeper reasons for the band's dissolution. While Mike was continuing to thrive musically with Snailhouse, Julien, by many accounts, was experiencing a profound disillusionment with his own sense of place as a musician and songwriter. "He has a very critical brain, and I think that created an edge to the way he related to what he was doing," says Tim Kingsbury. "He obviously loved doing it, but I think he was also very conflicted about it. He was pretty critical of himself... I remember him talking about being afraid that something he came up with sounded like The Zit Remedy"—the goofy, charmingly inept high-school band from the original *Degrassi* series. It's a funny reference, but a ridiculous comparison for Julien to make to his own deep and complex musical talent.

"Julien's so talented and wrote such beautiful songs, but it didn't seem like he really enjoyed himself doing music," says Julie Doiron with audible disappointment. "I don't think he felt it was a valid vocation. I was a little bummed and frustrated, but everybody has different priorities."

Julien himself cites more prosaic reasons for his estrangement from the music world. "The bottom line is there was no way for any of us to eke out a living," he says. "I think I would have been very happy—I probably still would be happy—eking out a living, but we just couldn't do that. For your mental health, you just can't keep flogging a dead horse."

In a February 2000 *Exclaim!* cover story on Julie Doiron and the Wooden Stars, touching on both their collaborative album and *The Moon*, Andrew described the reason for the band's continued existence as such: "No success (...) No money to talk about. We still enjoy playing together, and that's about all we have going for us. I don't mean to sound depressed—I'm not kidding. That's it."

Meanwhile, the band's latest label was also petering out. "I didn't want to make a living off music, I wanted to document something I thought was important," explains Alex Frenette. "The bands we were working with either broke up or got too big for us. Instead of continuing, we just went off to our own things." He moved to New York City to study, where he remains to this day, although his area of expertise isn't completely removed from his earlier work. In a bittersweet ironic twist, his dissertation is on what he describes as "labour patterns in the music industry: the rise and consequences of the unpaid intern economy—people working for free—and also the meaning people sustain from being in music."

Speaking of bittersweet irony, just as the band was winding down they received their greatest official honour, when *Julie Doiron and the Wooden Stars* won a Juno award for Best Alternative Album that spring. The only member of the band at the ceremony was Josh, who attended just for kicks; "everybody else thought it was a total waste of time because there was absolutely no chance we would win," he says. When they did in fact win, the genuinely bewildered bassist slowly made his way to the stage. The hosts, he recalls, "were looking at the security guards like 'should this guy be ejected?' because I was wearing a kung-fu outfit." He accepted the award with a speech including ape noises and a knock-knock joke.

In the *Exclaim!* story, writer James Keast introduced the band with this grim description: "It's hard to fathom that Wooden Stars are still together as a band. If the grinding gears of the music scene were going to chew up and spit out any group of sensitive, talented young men, it would be them." Unfortunately, that turned out to be an apt prophecy of exactly what would happen not long thereafter. "Some people decide they're okay with slugging it out and some people don't," says Doiron with resignation, "especially if they're smart and they can find other things to pay the bills." Within a year of their Juno victory, the band's leaders had left Ottawa—Julien had moved to Toronto to do his PhD, while Mike had decamped to Montreal—effectively putting an end to the band as a going concern.

CHAPTER 8

Come Back

"If you only have a 100 people in the world who care what you're doing, you don't have to call a press release every time you make a decision." –Michael Feuerstack

In 2001, my wife and I left Toronto for Montreal. Mocky and most of my other musical friends had moved to Europe, and after eight years in Toronto it felt like time for a change. Shortly after we got settled, I ran into Mike in a record store. I was going to record my own album in a studio soon, and though we barely knew each other, I impulsively asked him if he wanted to sing backup vocals on one of my songs. He said yes, and I was immediately excited but nervous. Although the people I was working with in the studio had trouble understanding this, it was as significant, and intimidating, to me as if an indie rock star on the level of Stephen Malkmus or Guided By Voices' Robert Pollard were sitting in.

But when Mike arrived at the studio, his presence put me at ease right away. Beloved in the music community as one of the nicest guys on the scene, he also had an open mind and good musical ideas. I'll always remember his advice when we had trouble finding the right harmony on one line. "When I can't find a harmony, I just don't do one," he said. Coming from one of the great harmonists, it seemed like wise counsel. He ended up singing and playing steel guitar on a number of my records.

During this time Mike continued to record and tour as Snailhouse, as well as performing with the Bell Orchestre (a chamber pop ensemble featuring Arcade Fire's Richard Parry and Sarah Neufeld), an early line-up of Nick Thorburn's Islands and multiple other collaborations. The other members of the Wooden Stars were much less active in music. At one point, there was even a rumour that Andrew had sold his drum kit. I saw him play once, when he came through town with my brother Nick and avant-jazz guitarist Justin Haynes, another Ottawa veteran. When we were hanging out I got up the courage to ask him, "So what's up with the Wooden Stars, is it officially over?" His response was an intriguing "Yes and no." Although he claimed unequivocally that "we'll never play together again," he also spoke about some incomplete recordings that the band wanted to finish in some form. I took that as a hopeful sign.

All the same, I couldn't help but notice that even the optimistic Mike had started to refer to the band in the past tense. And so I was surprised to find out a few years later that the band was reuniting. It was 2004, the same year that the Pixies got back together. I was even more excited about the Wooden Stars.

The band reunited at the request of Dave Draves, who asked them to play at his house for his 40th birthday party.

"They needed an excuse to get back together," Draves says. "Somebody else had to say to them, 'Guys, you need to give it another shot.' I don't think they felt they owed me anything, but I thought I could be the guy."

With typical contrariness, Mike denies that the breakup was a breakup, or the reunion a reunion. "In our mind, we had never really split up. I know that's absurd and I don't expect anybody to see it that way, but for us it wasn't really a reunion. If you only have a 100 people in the world who care what you're doing, you don't have to call a press release every time you make a decision," he laughs. "We weren't into it, so we didn't do it, and then when Dave asked us, that just seemed like enough impetus to bother dusting ourselves off and getting back together."

However, a little research reveals that a breakup might have been announced at some point; Mike told Hamilton's *View* magazine in 2005 that, "We only finally made the 'official breakup' announcement because we started to feel like dinks when we'd tell people that we were still a band but had nothing to show for it."

Whatever terminology you might use for the show at Draves's place, Mike recalls that "we had a lot of fun, and I think we realized that there was something special that we were missing." The band decided to play a few more shows and try to complete their unfinished material.

In February 2005 (luckily, by this point in the chronology the internet has stepped in to fill the gaps where memory fails), I saw the band for the third time at Montreal's cavernous, Thunderdome-like punk bar L'Hémisphère Gauche. The atmosphere was exciting. "I feel like a groupie!" exclaimed Mike's long-time girlfriend Katie. "Well, that's good," deadpanned Andrew, "because that's the closest thing to a groupie he's gonna get." Ever the businessman, Andrew then wandered the crowd counting heads, convinced that the promoter was short-changing the band on ticket sales.

The band hit the stage dressed from head to toe in white, displaying a heretofore untapped sense of showmanship. They ran through a series of songs from throughout their career. Audaciously, they did a totally straight cover of Pavement's hit "Cut Your Hair," with Mike cheekily quipping afterwards "I guess you can add Pavement to the list of bands that we've influenced."

Then Mathieu Beillard took the stage. Dressed in contrasting black, his slicked-back hair making him resemble a demented Pierce Brosnan, and cradling a glass of wine, he seemed to take on a smooth Vegas crooner persona as he sang the *Mardi Gras* classics "Hands to Work" and "Country Violins" with an ear-to-ear grin. Then, with Josh graciously stepping aside, Mathieu strapped on the bass to perform some of the proggier numbers from *The Very Same*. It was a truly magical show, the kind that gives fans more than they could ever expect.

Mathieu's participation in the reunion was short-lived. In the years after leaving the band, he'd done everything from studying physics to doing manual labour on a farm, but he'd recently found a new vocation, quite an unusual one for a former rock 'n' roller. Not long after the tour, he moved to Saskatchewan to undergo training with the RCMP.

That spring, the band were booked on a cross-country tour mounted by *Exclaim!*, the magazine that had always supported their efforts. Their presence on such a high-profile tour seemed to speak to their elder-statesman status, but they were out of place with such of-the-moment acts as Stars, the Organ and Montag. It was after one of these shows that a friend of mine who works in the music business referred to them as "not sexy"—a truly dick-shrivelling criticism if ever there was one, but perhaps fair enough in relative terms to the lusty Stars and the pouting all-girl Organ. And as Julien says with his usual inscrutable irony, "I suppose we were trying to be a rock band that had no sexual appeal to women."

"No one really knew who we were," recalls Andrew of the *Exclaim!* tour. "I think we were invited because a person booking the tour was a fan from back in the day. It was pretty awkward. The rooms were on the bigger side of what we would have done, ever. We were pretty out of it, we weren't really in game shape, so I don't think we were ready to capitalize on that opportunity or whatever. But it was still fun."

The reunion, however, wasn't intended to merely rehash the band's past glories. There was also the pesky matter of their incomplete "new" material. Both Andrew and Mike use the term "unfinished business" to describe the goals behind giving the band another shot. The Wooden Stars had another record in them.

CHAPTER 9

Gold Dust

"The Wooden Stars are just four strange guys who at various times didn't get along that well." –Andrew McCormack

In April 2007, I saw the Wooden Stars play live for the fourth and (to date) last time. This time around, my connection was personal—or rather, it almost was. A few days before the show, Andrew called me. The opening band had cancelled, and he asked if my band, The World Provider, would open for them.

After thinking about it for a day, I said no. My reasoning seems a bit inexplicable to me now. Walking the fine line between professional self-respect and artistic arrogance, I didn't want to play a show just because someone else had bailed out, with my name not even on the poster. Plus, I feared that with this last-minute offer, my band might not be in shape for such a prestigious slot. But today, when I think about turning down the opportunity to open for one of my all-time favourite bands, I always feel like kicking myself.

In front of an audience somewhat smaller than that for their reunion show (though heavily weighted with Arcade

Fire members), the band played a set with a lot of new material. The new songs were tight and muscular, generally upbeat and featuring a bit more swagger; I remember in one song both Mike and Julien kneeling to the floor to twiddle the knobs on their effects pedals, a bit of rock n' roll razzmatazz I wasn't expecting.

But in contrast to the joyous energy of the reunion set, this time the band seemed a bit uneasy onstage. In one song, Julien shouted "I hate you all"; I was relieved to later learn that this was an actual lyric, not a spontaneous outcry towards the crowd (which it seemed like). At the end of the set, Mike came out onstage for an encore, then stood at the mic making awkward jokes for an agonizingly long time until the other members could be coaxed onstage. It was highly uncomfortable. Still, the new songs sounded great, with the singing, lyrics and musicianship in better form than ever. That night, I picked up their new record, *People Are Different*, at the merch table.

With many of its songs dating from before the hiatus, in a sense *People Are Different* is less a collection of new material than a clearing out of the band's catalogue. Julie Doiron remembers closing track "Clouds" being part of the Wooden Stars' set when they first toured together in the mid-late 90s, while Dave Draves states that, "I don't think I would be ridiculous in saying they wrote two new songs in the 2000s."

Looking back, almost as much time elapsed between the reunion and *People Are Different* as the band had spent on hiatus beforehand. While Mike continued to stay active with Snailhouse and his various team-player efforts, the other members made occasional musical appearances amid the demands of their everyday lives.

In his only other musical showcase to date, Julien collaborated in a duo with guitarist and fellow Ottawa expat Justin Haynes. Entitled Men In Love, the project produced a self-released album in 2005. If ever a fan wanted a stark demonstration of the differences between the Wooden Stars' two songwriters, they could listen to the quiet and contemplative songwriting of Snailhouse next to the challenging, resolutely avant-garde (but still beautiful) instrumental guitar music of Men In Love.

The project also illustrated Julien's penchant for deliberate obscurity. Aside from the project name and song titles—which range from misanthropic inside jokes ("If Women Counted," "Bring Back Shame") to songs that appear to be covers ("House of the Rising Sun," "When a Man Loves a Woman") but in fact are the same in name only, to the opener perversely titled "Wooden Stars"—the CD booklet contains not a single piece of information, not even the members' names.

Men In Love performed a single show, at Toronto's long-running indie concert series Wavelength. When asked to do an interview for the Wavelength zine and website, Julien submitted a bizarre and incoherent essay, supposedly an unaltered assignment by one of his philosophy students. The anonymous zine editor added, in a frustrated editorial comment, "I mean, come on!... but okay, this was pretty funny."

Another excursion was even further under the radar. I had the privilege, unfortunately shared by very few, of seeing Julien and Andrew back up Mocky when he returned from Europe for two shows in Montreal and Quebec City in 2006. Though the attendance at these shows was tragically poor, the performances by this power trio of Ottawa veterans was memorable. Mocky's song "So Sorry," which would appear a year later as the opening track of Feist's breakthrough album *The Reminder*, sounded great with Julien's guitar and vocal harmonies.

In the years following the reunion, the Wooden Stars collaborated in fits and starts, eventually laying down bed tracks (drums, bass and elementary guitars) for an album at Toronto's Halla Music studio. But between their day jobs, geographical disparity and ongoing artistic head-butting, the songs continued to linger unfinished.

In a funny sort of coming full circle, the album was completed with the help of Peter Murray, Julien and Mathieu's cousin who had kickstarted their career way back by introducing them to their future manager. Murray, a professional musician who's played with artists ranging from respected singer-songwriter Ron Sexsmith to 80s rockers Honeymoon Suite as well as dabbling in production and his own original music, had followed the Wooden Stars' career with interest.

"I did live sound for them a few times," he recalls, "and was sort of peripherally involved in advising them on various matters—encouraging them to get [guitar] tuners and stuff like that, trying to encourage their professional development." Like most of their fans, he was impressed with their musicianship—"They were sort of in this 1990s Canadian indie rock scene, but their musical ideas and in fact their musical abilities were pretty far beyond their colleagues"—as well as their originality. "There's not a lot of clichés in their music, and on the rare times there are, they're pretty much tongue-in-cheek."

Murray now saw the band struggling to finish their album. "They still had that connection," he says, "but they were discouraged by how difficult it was to get together... and as pretty much anyone involved in original music in Canada knows, it's not easy on a practical level to make things work."

After a family cottage get-together, Murray remembers, "I remember driving with Julien and listening to the bed tracks with him. I said 'You guys really need to finish this record. You're such a great band, and it'd be a shame if this didn't get completed.' I probably offered to help them at that point."

Murray took on a production role, completing the recording with Julien and Mike at his own home studio. "It was just a matter of drawing them out a bit more," he says of his producer role. "I felt that a lot of their ideas were coming across a little too humbly, perhaps. I know the indie rock aesthetic often includes a certain amount of self-effacement. And a certain amount of that can be charming. But I think one of the things that was starting to come through even in the bed track sessions was a greater level of confidence and more of a rock element. In terms of the vibe, I wanted to encourage more balls, more rock."

This confidence comes through in all aspects of the album, from the upbeat tempos and muscular drumming to the clear, forceful vocals to the guitar playing; several songs include previously unheard elements like effects pedals and solos that occasionally come close to outright shredding. When recording was complete, the whole band gathered to supervise the mix at Toronto's Phase One studio. "It was a bit of a revelation to the band working at Phase One, which is one of the best studios in the country," says Murray.

The album starts off with the upbeat "Orphans." While Mike and Julien's harmonies are instantly recognizable, the music has undergone another mutation. The stereo-panned guitars play tight down- and upstrokes, almost resembling ska (except not horrible), while Andrew's fiercely fast drumming evokes the "disco punk" beat that was briefly trendy around that time.

With the briefest pause, the album then continues with the equally fast-paced "Pretty Girl." Julien's lyrics combine another cynical take on the music business with a stalker's ode a shade darker than "Every Breath You Take": *Viral strains of the radio. When the halfwit sings, I'll follow you and I don't care what you think you want, or who.* Toronto jazz saxophonist (and member of the Broken Social Scene empire) David French joins in at the end, but unlike the free blowing found on the first two albums, here the horn part is a tight, double-tracked melodic line. This opening one-two punch makes it clear that the band is going for a different feeling than on the downbeat *The Moon*.

Another aspect of the band that comes to the forefront on *People Are Different* is their absurdist sense of humour, especially notable after the understated and melancholy feel of *The Moon*. "Orphans" opens with lines rhyming *We are little orphans* with *Depleting our endorphins*, and ends with the declaration *We're putting the heart back in heart attack*. "Last Secret Infirmary" finds Julien and Mike belting *You don't give a rat's ass for progress when you're working in a foundry. In a barber's chair with my mule's hair, picaresque liaisons disappoint me.* (Only the Wooden Stars could make those lines actually catchy). "Boating Accident," perhaps the most joyfully ridiculous song in the band's discography, includes everything from proto-LOLspeak (*We did it because of we had poverty*) to old-fashioned heroics (*The Coast Guard made men of us all*) to, most unexpectedly, hip hop cliché (*Waving their arms in the air. They wave them like they just don't care*).

But the band could still turn around and be as poignant as they were absurd. "Gold Dust," the album's closest thing to a ballad, is one of their very best songs. (Disclosure obliges me to note that my brother Nick makes a barely audible cameo at the song's start, playing a soft snare pattern with brush sticks—the only element to make the cut from what he remembers as a session of laying down "a bunch of really crazy shit" on various tracks).

Sung by Julien over an understated track (which only upon a close listen turns out to be in one of the band's maddeningly complex time signatures), the lyrics begin with probably the subtlest version of the band's recurring theme of violent menace—*Fragments of the setting sun, they said it was an accident. In the crosshairs, having fun, hated*—and wrap up with some of their strongest imagery: *Gold dust settles in the whites of your eyes. You say you only believe in love, but I only believe in fire*. The song concludes with a Brian Wilson-worthy coda of harmonic *ooohs*.

At last, the record was released on a proper label, Hamilton's stalwart indie Sonic Unyon. Mainly a distributor (who'd carried *Mardi Gras*), Sonic Unyon occasionally released records by bands they particularly believed in. The CD had a great cover, a 3D collage of the band members' faces by Andrew's sister Katie McCormack and her artist partner Philippe Blanchard. While the title comes from a longstanding band joke about their inability to reach a larger audience—"People are different is a phrase we have used for years to justify our own existence," Andrew told *View* magazine's Shain Shapiro in 2007—it also alludes to the band's uneasy peace with their internal differences, and the artwork brilliantly captures the awkward but beautiful fit between them.

Although more than one person I spoke to considers *People Are Different* the band's best album, others find it overproduced. "They wanted to make it the studio album they'd never made, really exact and no compromises," says Draves. "I don't know what their ideal fan wants from them, but personally I like it when they're more edgy than refined. I just think 'don't overwork it.'" And although Draves freely admits that he may feel this way because the band chose to work with a producer other than him, he's not alone in this view.

Personally, I think it's great that all four albums sound so different from each other, and although I enjoy the madness of the early records, it's also cool to hear the band experimenting with studio refinement. I can understand why some of their old school fans find the production of *People Are Different* over the top—the indie mentality prizes a loose approach and decries any kind of gloss. But with the high energy and humour from the band's beginnings, and the perfectionism and pop sensibility of *The Moon*, the album can also be seen as the best of both worlds for a Wooden Stars fan.

Draves suggests that the band may have been inspired by their friends' success to shoot for the big time. "With Jeremy and the Arcade Fire, I think they got the feeling that people were ready to hear something challenging again. But they were never that band," he says. "In the end, they were prepared for anything to happen because they thought they missed their shot. But I don't think they were ever gonna be a popular band."

Andrew dismisses the notion that the band were aiming for either commercial success or a long-term career. "It was really only supposed to be a one-time deal anyway—make a record, play a few shows. I don't think we had any delusions about going any further than that," he says. But in a 2007 interview with *Exclaim!*'s Vish Khanna, Andrew had suggested otherwise while talking about *People Are Different*'s slicker sound. "It's likely the endpoint for that particular path, as the Wooden Stars look toward the future," he said, going on to tantalizingly suggest that the band might return to a more experimental direction.

While completing *People Are Different*, the band also recorded a Rheostatics cover, "Saskatchewan," for a tribute album. Although the band occasionally covered other artists in concert, this is their only cover song on record (for the curious, it can be heard on the band's last.fm page, and also comes as a bonus track with *People Are Different* when downloaded from Canadian digital distributor Zunior). As with the Julie Doiron album, it's fascinating to hear the band take on another artist's material, and the Rheos' emotionally charged Canadiana is given a twist by Julien's vocal performance, finding him in full command of his late-period mastery of melancholy.

When I saw their spring 2007 show, it seemed that the band's personal differences were once again getting in the way of their momentum. But they still had one more kick at the can. When I'd seen them in 2005, the opening act was an indie-ish rock band called Wintersleep. I didn't find them particularly memorable, but two years later they'd become quite popular, and decided to return the favour by taking the Wooden Stars as their opener on a cross-country tour.

"Humbling" is how Andrew describes the Wintersleep tour. "As generous as it was of those guys to bring us out on the road," he says, "we would be in some strange place and we'd sell like two copies of the record and one shirt to my aunt or something. And then they'd sell like 300 records and 400 shirts. The crowd would be going absolutely crazy for them. At some point, it was like 'okay, this is not necessarily making a lot of sense,' even though we had fun playing together."

Andrew also had an epiphany about the Wooden Stars being "not really on the same page" when he observed Wintersleep's internal relations. "Having toured with them for a month, it was just clear that they were compatible and committed to their project collectively," he says. "The Wooden Stars are just four strange guys who at various times didn't get along that well. There wasn't enough collective teamwork or whatever, that you really have to have to be in a band. It's like being on a sports team—it's a bad analogy, but it's kind of true. You have to have the same playbook every once in a while."

The tour also coincided with the birth of Josh's daughter, who was only three weeks old when they headed on the road—making the outing, as he puts it, "necessarily a swan song" for his touring commitments.

And so the band members went back to their day jobs and individual lives. Like their first break, it was less a dramatic finish than a naturally occurring drift apart. And as Julien asks, not entirely rhetorically: "What else are we gonna do?"

CHAPTER 10

Clouds

"For a while, it was this perfect little club that you'd wanna be in if you were a little kid, with its own secret language." –Julien Beillard

The Wooden Stars were a critically acclaimed band, widely acknowledged as masterful musicians and songwriters. They inspired utter devotion among their followers and directly inspired many musicians, including Arcade Fire, the single most successful indie rock act of the 21st century to date.

That band's Jeremy Gara says that in his travels, he's seen that the Wooden Stars' influence goes beyond Canadian borders. "A lot of people who I really like know their music, well beyond what I would have thought. Lots of American cool indie rock bands cite them as an influence," he says. "They're a songwriters' band, which is a great compliment for those who receive it, but it's also a curse in a weird way."

It does sometimes seem that the Wooden Stars were cursed. Perhaps it would be overstating the case to call them the Canadian equivalent of Big Star, Alex Chilton's legendary power pop group who influenced a whole generation of musicians but, through a combination of bad luck and self-sabotage, never made it beyond cult status. But in a similar vein, the Wooden Stars' importance and influence stubbornly remained disproportionate to their actual success. I always figured they were destined for greatness, but it never happened, and I often wondered why.

In the process of speaking to people for this book, a number of theories came up to explain this Canadian rock tragedy.

HYPOTHESIS ONE: THE MUSIC WAS TOO DEMANDING

Amy Hersenhoren: "They weren't writing straight pop songs. It was challenging music, which is a good thing, but not everybody can get their head around that, right? The early stuff always erred on the side of strange. You'll have a beautiful pop melody with great guitars going on, and then all of a sudden they'll break down into some weird freakout. And I think that was beyond a lot of people, plain and simple."

Samir Khan: "They asked a lot of an audience. If you were willing to pay attention, they would bring rich rewards from repeated listening. But you'd always have to be comfortable with the confusion they would instil in your heart. Some people will get it, but a general musical audience is not looking for that kind of experience. They're looking for something that they can dance to, or pump a fist to, or to play in the background to their brunch. Or maybe their conception of 'difficult' is different than mine."

Wyatt Boyd: "Have you ever tried to tap your foot along to a 5/4 beat? It's not for everyone. Girls do not dance to their music. Their sound is more geared towards the heart and mind than it is towards the feet, and the winnowing effect this had on their audience (both boys and girls alike) is not to be underestimated."

Tim Kingsbury: "It's autistic pop music. There's something underneath, it's hard to read the face of it."

HYPOTHESIS TWO: WRONG PLACE, WRONG TIME

Wyatt Boyd: "Had Wooden Stars been making music a little bit earlier or a little bit later they would probably have stood a better chance. Think of something like [Talking Heads'] *Fear of Music* (1979): that was a gold record in its day!"

Amy Hersenhoren: "It was tough to get heard if you were up here in the 90s. It was a bit of a different thing for a Canadian band to be heard. There was no Pitchfork then. There was no internet! I honestly do feel that if they were making records longer into the time that the internet existed, that things would have been a little bit different for them. They were a victim of the technology of the time."

Andrew McCormack: "The Canadian indie rock market in 1997 was just not a mature market. And there's some real challenges to playing music in Canada. To play 30 shows, you have to drive halfway around the world and back. That's really hard to do. It's draining, it's exhausting, it's insane."

Mocky: "I don't know about that, but they only could have come from Canada."

HYPOTHESIS THREE: THEY BLEW THEIR ONE SHOT AT SUCCESS WITH SUB POP

Geoffrey Pye: "The unfortunate truth is they were being kind of stupid, thinking they didn't need anything like that. Maybe if you're swept up in a real moment of creativity and inspiration that's how you're supposed to feel, but in retrospect I'm sure it was a poor choice. Their music would have reached so many more people."

Samir Khan: "There are sometimes second chances in rock and roll, but I feel like those are largely a figment of a more forgiving time in the past. It may not have even existed. They thought they'd have another kick at it when they were ready. They didn't."

HYPOTHESIS FOUR (RELATED TO HYPOTHESIS THREE): SELF-SABOTAGE THROUGH BEING DIFFICULT ARTISTS

Dave Draves: "They were one of the bands I know that was their own worst enemy. Things would come up that were good opportunities and Julien would say no. They were dismissive of anyone who wasn't—not cool necessarily, 'cause they were never that cool. They were a certain way, and they didn't want anybody who didn't understand that to be involved."

Jeremy Gara: "They're the strongest of characters, which is why their music is so great, but they're really weird people."

HYPOTHESIS FIVE (RELATED TO HYPOTHESES THREE AND FOUR): ARTISTIC INTEGRITY

Jeremy Gara: "They didn't pander. They were punk as fuck. They weren't going to compromise their music for anything, and that's a hard place to start if you're gonna break on through and make a living at it."

Peter Murray: "The people who become big stars, it's rarely by accident. There's usually a fair amount of deliberate effort to get there. And that does include a lot of very pragmatic decisions, artistic and otherwise. The Wooden Stars guys are real artists. Like many musicians, they probably fell through the cracks of wanting success and wanting to do what they wanted to do. You want some level of success. But the question is, how many compromises do you want to make? People who have any artistic integrity at all are gonna draw the line somewhere, but they will flirt with that line. I don't know that the Wooden Stars really compromised at all."

Some, most or all of these hypotheses may be true. I sometimes feel that a line from their first album, *My innocent gears defeat me well*, contained an accidental self-fulfilling prophecy. But there's a bottom line, which Tim Kingsbury sums up succinctly when asked why the Wooden Stars never broke through: "Most bands don't." Without directly referring to his own band's massive success, he continues: "There really has to be a lot of luck, if you're blessed with this idea that works externally. And you can't predict that; you can't even take credit for it, really."

And when it came to luck, the Wooden Stars' was quite simply chronically bad. Of their four records, three were put out on labels that folded soon after. (And unlike labels in the decimated music business of today, they didn't even have file-sharing to blame). Around the time of the reunion, Andrew told me about being contacted by someone at the EMI warehouse, who explained that the remaining CDs of *The Very Same* would be destroyed unless the band wanted to buy them back. They chose to split the difference, buying back as many as they could afford to and seeing the rest go to a landfill—an event truly brutal in its symbolism.

But regardless of material success or the lack thereof, the band members are all philosophical and at peace with the role the band has played in their lives. "We made some pretty weird music, and we had a surprisingly big audience," says Mike. "I feel really proud of all the music that we did, that's the main thing. We did a lot of really good shows. We treated each other well, for the most part," he laughs. "I don't think I've laughed harder with any other group of people in my life."

Prodded further about the band's career, Mike gently corrects me: "It's an art project, it's not a career. So yeah, I guess I'm happy from that perspective. And I haven't really changed that perspective in everything else that I do. Even though I'm trying to get by, it's always an art project."

Today, Julien Beillard is a professor of philosophy at Ryerson University in Toronto. Since the Wooden Stars' last effort he's dabbled in music occasionally—recording demos with Geoff Pye, playing a bit with Samir Khan's band Tusks, and even joining Mike onstage at a Snailhouse show in Toronto in 2011. But the only music he plays these days is jamming on toy instruments with his young daughter. He still looks back with fondness on the band. "Maybe the best thing about the whole experience, looking back on it, was that for a while, it was this perfect little club that you'd wanna be in if you were a little kid, with its own secret language."

Andrew McCormack is currently a solar energy entrepreneur, also based in Toronto and also the father of a young son. "I always dream of playing again, it's just a matter of making the time to seek out people and make the connections again," he says. "It's hard to go hang out in the cool bars with interesting musicians when you have to change diapers and wipe vomit off your shirt on a regular basis." Despite his generally cynical point of view on his experiences in the business side of music, he's quick to add: "Certainly no regrets. I'm really thankful that I had the chance to have music be part of my upbringing. I met some lifelong friends and really interesting, smart, perhaps slightly crazy people. It's informed a lot of my life, what I do and how I see things. That's really good, but I don't think of it as a success per se," he adds with a rueful laugh. "It's just what happened in my life."

Josh Latour is a farmer, builder and father of two kids near Perth, Ontario. He occasionally plays live shows in the area with local bluegrass jams and cover bands. "As hard as touring was for us (financially, physically, mentally), I have to say that I'll never trade those times in for anything other," he writes in our brief email exchange. "I love those guys (and Julie too)."

Mathieu Beillard is an RCMP officer stationed in Fort McMurray, Alberta. "I suppose I will always regret quitting a bit," admits the onetime wild card of the band, whose musical pursuits since moving on have been limited to on-again, off-again endeavours to learn various instruments. "I feel a little nostalgic about it at times, especially when I listen to one of the records. It was an exciting and especially creative time in my life. I sometimes even now miss the band practices and playing gigs. Playing with the Wooden Stars was a great experience and I'm proud of all the music that we made."

After 17 years performing as Snailhouse, Michael Feuerstack retired the project name and continues to record and tour under his own name, as well as playing guitar with the Luyas, the Bell Orchestre and various other artists. As I write this, he is about to release a new album, *Tambourine Death Bed*, and spend the year touring. "Nobody's, like, slugging it out anymore, except for me," he reflects on his former bandmates. Then, breaking into one of the many laughs that punctuate our interview, he exclaims: "Somebody's gotta represent the Wooden Stars in this crazy world!"

Since Mike was so adamant that the breakup was not in fact a breakup, I can't help but ask: are the band just on another undefined hiatus; is there more Wooden Stars music in the future? "I feel like circumstances are so different now that it's unlikely," he says, choosing his words carefully. "But if someone wants to organize something, I'll totally show up."

Somewhat to my surprise, Julien leaves the same door open a crack. "I would love to find a way to do more music, or even to play with those guys again if we could, but it doesn't seem feasible right now," he laughs before drawing an unexpected comparison. "I was checking my email, and in the MSN news feed it said 'Coldplay announces three-year hiatus,'" he recalls, pausing to contemplate the odd nature of what constitutes a news item in the digital age. "I suppose if you told Coldplay 'make another record and we'll give you the entire South Pacific as your private fiefdom,' maybe they would do it. But within the world that's available to them, there's not much more they can do.

"And I guess in our small way, it was a bit like that. We like playing music, but we're getting old, and we just don't have enough money coming from anywhere to finance playing music in a way that is even moderately acceptable or tolerable for guys in their late thirties. Like, if we wanted to go on tour again, we'd be camping in a van and could probably only afford a single room at the Super 8, sneaking in the last guy. You can do that when you're 19, but at our age it's just too bleak to contemplate, so that's all it is."

Julien addresses a topic that a lot of music fans may not fully grasp, but that any indie musician knows all too well (though few of us have the candour to discuss it publicly). With the exception of a very, very few success stories, devoting yourself to a musician's life is akin to taking a vow of poverty. Unless you're independently wealthy, ruthlessly ambitious, extraordinarily lucky or some combination of the above, you have to live a lifestyle that's only few steps above that of a homeless person, subsisting on very little and stretching sporadic bursts of income over long periods of time. Either that, or get a day job and resign yourself to treating music as an expensive and time-consuming hobby that may spend long stretches on the back burner. It's a difficult decision, one I'm intimately familiar with. Being chronically broke has a certain romanticism in your twenties, much less so as you approach middle age. So you can hardly blame someone for choosing to put this life aside.

If it's true that the Wooden Stars music is an acquired taste, the flip side of that is that after all these years (not to mention the intense, concentrated listening required to write this book), I feel like I still discover new things to appreciate every time I hear them. It doesn't just hold up well; I actually enjoy it more the more I listen.

I love this band. And if you're a huge music nerd—which, if you've read this far, you must be—I bet you would too.

As a fan, I can't help but be a bit frustrated that they never broke through, but maybe that's not the right way to look at it. In our interview, Jeremy Gara reminded me of something important: "If you can write songs as great as they did, that's definitely a success."

Because in the end, money and status are as fleeting as the clouds—rolling in, floating away. But not music. It lives on regardless, magical, infectious, ours.

THE BIBLIOPHONIC SERIES is a catalogue of the ongoing history of contemporary music. Each book is a time capsule, capturing artists and their work as we see them, providing a unique look at some of today's most exciting musicians.